Praise for *Glamour Witch*

"*Glamour Witch* is the perfect book for anyone who wants to learn the powerful magic that beauty and seduction offer."
—Sarah Lyons (@citymystic), author of *How to Study Magic* and *Revolutionary Witchcraft*

"A dynamic and provocative work on the power of bewitchment with aesthetics . . . must-read for anyone looking to add beauty, fashion, and adornment to their magical practice."
—Michael Herkes, author of *The GLAM Witch* and *Glamcraft*

"Sophie Saint Thomas is without a doubt one of the most glamorous, enchanting witches anyone could ever meet. Her guide to style and beauty is not to be missed!"
—Annabel Gat, author of *The Astrology of Love and Sex* and *The Moon Sign Guide*

Glamour Witch

Glamour Witch

CONJURING STYLE & GRACE
TO GET WHAT YOU WANT

SOPHIE SAINT THOMAS

WEISER
BOOKS

This edition first published in 2023 by Weiser Books, an imprint of Red Wheel/Weiser, LLC
With offices at:
65 Parker Street, Suite 7
Newburyport, MA 01950
www.redwheelweiser.com

ISBN: 978-1-57863-775-1
Library of Congress Cataloging-in-Publication Data available upon request.

Cover and text design by Sky Peck Design
Cover photograph © Getty Images
Interior images by Milatoo
Typeset in Adobe Jensen Pro

Printed in the United States of America
IBI

10 9 8 7 6 5 4 3 2 1

This book is dedicated to Dr. Chad Johnson
and his red leather tie.

CONTENTS

Acknowledgments

Thank you to my beloved friends, although I wish you were more honest with me during some of my more questionable hair decisions. Thanks to my father for your dapper suits and teaching me about Erno Laszlo. To my mother, who once flew out of a hurricane zone with my sister and me wearing an evening gown because it was all that the storm didn't blow away. Many thanks to my plastic surgeon Dr. Dara Liotta for the best rhinoplasty a girl could ask for. Thank you to my dearest agent, Eric Smith, and my publisher, Weiser Books, for seeing my glamorous vision to the end. Many thanks to Chad, my man and forever muse, for always inspiring me to be beautiful. Thanks to David Bowie, Freddie Mercury, Dita Von Teese, and the glamour witches before me. To the Virgin Islands, where I grew up, and, of course, thank you to my grown-up home, New York City, which will always be the most glamorous place on Earth.

INTRODUCTION

Young David Bowie isn't particularly panty-dropping. In 1964, he wasn't even David Bowie, but Davie Jones, a snaggletoothed British wannabe pop star whose most glamorous moment was forming the "Society for the Prevention of Cruelty to Men with Long Hair."

Now, however, the David Bowie that comes to mind whenever we say his adopted name is a panty-dropper regardless of your gender or what type of underwear you have on. Bowie turned himself into an icon with a slight name change, orange hair dye, androgynous costume, and music meant to be blasted into outer space. "Even though I was very shy, I found I could get on stage if I had a new identity," the Starman once said. While the hair and bulge-enhancing trousers certainly helped, Bowie's charisma and confidence sold the show. Beauty is subject to genetics and societal expectations—but glamour is a skill. This book will teach you how to use it.

The word *glamour* originally meant "to cast a spell"; it was an illusion created by witches. Over the years, the term evolved. Its magickal origins were forgotten as it became a synonym for elegance and beauty. We still see portrayals of glamour magick in modern film and television. In the 1996 film *The Craft*, Neve Campbell's character changes her hair color in an instant. Now, I can't teach you how to bleach your hair with nothing but your fingertips. But I can tell you how to dye your hair Ziggy Stardust orange in an hour—a feat that would undoubtedly get you burned at the stake for witchcraft in eighteenth-century Scotland when *glamour* translated directly to witchcraft.

In *Game of Thrones*, the Red Woman Melisandre is a beautiful witch capable of bending the will of men. Matching her red hair and clothing is a ruby necklace. The story line reveals that once Melisandre takes off the necklace, she shows her true form: a shriveled aging woman, or in other words, the fiercest of crones. The charmed choker created a glamour to gain power by manipulating societal ageism and men's weak spot: sex. Now, you can't take decades off with a necklace. Still, we use red stones such as ruby and garnet to summon love and lust, just as orange represents the creativity and eccentricity we find in Ziggy Stardust. (Don't worry—this book comes with a complete color magick section.) And let's not forget the existence of Botox, a continuously controversial, yet indisputably effective way to remove wrinkles, should one desire. Just like you'd be burned at the stake for a bottle of Manic Panic hair dye, your plastic surgeon would have been convicted of witchcraft back in the day. Glamour allows your inside to match your outside.

But back to Bowie. He didn't only knock it out of the park with his glamour skills, but the Starman knew how to choose a wife. On April 4, 1992, Bowie married the Somali American model Iman. "My attraction to her was immediate and all-encompassing," Bowie told *Hello!* in 2000, according to Biography.com.[1]

Iman was discovered by photographer Peter Beard, who helped launch her career but also created a racist mythology about the woman he viewed as his Somali protégé. Beard claimed that she was the child of a goatherd he had stumbled across in the African bush while, in reality, Iman is a diplomat's daughter educated at boarding schools in Cairo and at the University of Nairobi. "I was not 'lost' to be discovered in a jungle," Iman told the *New York Times.* "I've never been in a jungle in my life!"[2]

After two decades of struggling with makeup artists trying to match her skin tone backstage at runway shows in her career as a supermodel, Iman created her own skin care line, Iman Cosmetics, in 1994. The line included shades for all skin tones and opened doors for future Black beauty entrepreneurs such as Rihanna, whose Fenty Beauty offers fifty shades of foundation. Unfortunately, mainstream glamour industries have a record of dismissing those who are different, just as historically, marginalized folks were targeted in witch hunts.

After Bowie died, Iman created her first fragrance—Love Memoir. Love Memoir smells of bergamot, rose, and Bowie's favorite vetiver. The warm,

ambery vetiver, derived from a plant similar to lemongrass, is now found in fragrances such as Paris Hilton Heiress and Prada Infusion de Vetiver. However, long before fashion labels and reality stars caught on, witches have been using vetiver, also known as "the oil of tranquility," in spells for processing grief and curating calm. So one must wonder—did Iman sense these magickal properties when crafting a scent in memory of her husband?

In the pages that follow, you'll realize that you're likely already practicing glamour magick, such as taking a lavender-infused bath to unwind. Of course, if you're a Pisces, your bath game is likely already strong. But, to give everyone an educated introduction to witchcraft, we'll talk about tarot, astrology, color magick, and more—all from a glamorous perspective. For instance, you'll learn that the Five of Wands can act as a reminder that just because all your friends are shaving their heads to embrace a queer identity doesn't mean that you have to. You're still just as gay with long hair.

The LGBTQIA+ community is crucial in witchcraft and fashion history, from those killed during the Salem witch trials for suspected lesbianism to gay icon Alexander McQueen's stunning autumn/winter 1995–96 tartan collection *Highland Rape*—which is a reference to English colonialism, not literal rape. Therefore, we'll be ensuring that you're up to date with modern queer terminology and know about gender nonconforming deities such as Dionysus, the god of wine and orgies.

This book also includes sections on the rich histories of the glamour industries—skin care, clothing, body modifications, etc. You'll learn what Botox and nightshade have in common and what Hollywood did to actors before the facelift was perfected. While Hitler literally wrote rules against makeup, in countries such as Korea a proper skin care regime has always been considered a critical part of health—including for men. These chapters dive into everything from fashion to body piercing from the witch's perspective and how beauty, war, and sex are intertwined.

In the spell chapters of this book, you'll not only learn that glamour is power, but also how to wield it to your advantage. We'll talk about post-breakup haircuts that include a cord-cutting ritual, how to find fashion inspiration from ancestors, and magickal manicures using charms and color magick to attract marriage. Because regardless of who you are . . . you are just as glamorous as David Bowie, and you deserve to find your Iman.

All the rumors are true. Vanity is a sin . . . and a very delicious one at that.

PART ONE

Glamour 101

1

FINISHING SCHOOL

Before we get started, there are a few things that every glamour witch should know. And don't worry: a rebellious spirit is welcome at Glamour Witch Finishing School. After all, the infamous magician Johann Georg Faust of Germany, who allegedly sold his soul to the devil, understood the magick in *grammatica*, the word *glamour* originates from. The connection to today's idea of grammar—that is, language—remains. Language is knowledge, and the occult is sacred, and often hidden, knowledge. But times are changing, and you must adapt or die.

While in eighteenth-century England, a man could be imprisoned for wearing makeup, today, thanks to social media, beauty boys like Patrick Starrr are teaching the rest of us how to keep up. Likewise, in addition to makeup trends, TikTok's witch community is the go-to place for daily tarot readings and astrology, two subjects that, once upon a time, only a lucky few had access to. So let's briefly dive into the history of glamour, complete with a decade-by-decade fashion timeline, because you know some art hoe might ask you about Lana Del Rey's flower crown and you can say that Marsha P. Johnson wore it first. And if it weren't for the violence and rationing of World War II, we wouldn't have the bikini, and without Vivienne Westwood's shop SEX on London's King's Road, we wouldn't have ads for high-end safety pin earrings flooding our timelines.

Glamour Witch Finishing School also includes discussions on gender and orientation, complete with easy-to-reference guides on related terminology. Of course, we live in a time of gender revolution and are constantly adjusting our language to keep up. So I apologize in advance if anything included becomes outdated or I missed something. Unlike J. K. Rowling, I promise I did my best and always strive to be better. Because while colonialism may still be clinging to the gender binary, if we want to talk about history, gender nonconforming folks have historically been accepted as sacred. Simply look at the two-spirit people from Indigenous North American tribes or the hijras of India.

And, while we're at it, if it weren't for queer folks, we wouldn't have the danceable fabrics created by Roy Halston Frowick that draped the sweaty bodies inside Studio 54. Likewise, without the LGBTQIA+ community, we wouldn't get to cheer for Pierre Davis of the genderless fashion label No Sesso—which is Italian for "No Sex/No Gender." Davis became the first trans person to present at New York Fashion Week during the Fall 2020 season. Later, we'll combine our modern and inclusive fashion knowledge, throw it into the cauldron with some old-fashioned witchcraft, and brew up some spells.

Origins of Glamour

Glamour (n.)

1720, Scottish, "magic, enchantment" (especially in phrase to cast the glamor), a variant of Scottish gramarye "magic, enchantment, spell," said to be an alteration of English grammar (q.v.) in a specialized use of that word's medieval sense of "any sort of scholarship, especially occult learning," the latter sense attested from c. 1500 in English but said to have been more common in Medieval Latin. Popularized in English by the writings of Sir Walter Scott (1771–1832). Sense of "magical beauty, alluring charm" first recorded in 1840. As that quality of attractiveness especially associated with Hollywood, high-fashion, celebrity, etc., by 1939.

Source: Online Etymology Dictionary[3]

They say that beauty is in the eye of the beholder. It's true that different people have different types, and there's no denying that beauty standards are subject to genetics and societal forces. But glamour, darling, is entirely in your control. Some people are born with perfectly chiseled jawlines; others grow epic beards. Some of us have naturally symmetric noses; others learn to contour, get rhinoplasties or lean into our noses with the grace of Barbra Streisand or else risk the fate of Cyrano de Bergerac. Can you imagine how different the romantic's life would have been had he owned that nose from the very beginning? Based on a real person, this character was an epically talented writer—and frankly, pretty hot. Who doesn't love a guy with a nose that could bash in skulls? But he let his insecurities prevent him from living his best life and getting the girl.

Such self-limiting behavior is unacceptable, witches. It is your responsibility to honor your talents and desirability. Yes, Beyoncé is talented, but her glamour is also evident in her devotion to perfection established through practice, practice, and more practice. "Power means happiness, power means hard work and sacrifice,"[4] she told *Billboard* in 2011. Yes, in case you are wondering, she is a Virgo. The Queen B is flawless, but that magick took hard work and a lot of self-love. "The world will see you the way you see you and treat you the way you treat yourself,"[5] the icon told *Elle* in 2016. Glamour magick, like all magick, comes from within. And sometimes, it comes with the aid of some sorcery.

Glamour is how a blonde Michigan-born stripper became the raven-haired Dita Von Teese, whose signature beauty mark is actually a tattoo. And as for that body? Dita says that not only does she do Pilates each morning, but she tries to have sex if she can, too! Her famous blue-black hair comes from a bottle, the perfect porcelain skin aided by religious use of sunscreen, and her signature red lip is a staple she won't leave home without wearing. And she does it all herself, even using affordable products. According to her manifesto *Your Beauty Mark: The Ultimate Guide to Eccentric Glamour*, with an eight-dollar box of Nutrisse Ultra-Color Blue Black and a three-dollar tube of Wet n Wild Red Velvet, anyone can rock Dita-approved glamour for minimal expense.[6]

The word *glamour* comes from Scotland. In the early 1700s, the Scottish adjusted the English word *grammar* to *glamour*, with the definition being "a magic spell." But even before then, notable magicians—such as the aforementioned Johann Georg Faust of Germany—associated the word *grammatica* with occult learning. Knowledge is power, and at the time, using astrology, spells, and other forms of witchcraft was accepted as part of learning, which the word *grammatica* referred to. The occult references hidden knowledge, after all. Faust allegedly died in an explosion of an alchemical experiment, so gruesome it was assumed the devil had come to collect his mutilated body. According to legend, and as depicted in Johann Wolfgang von Goethe's 1808 drama *Faust*, the man did wish to sell his soul to the devil. In the mid-1800s, the word *glamour* began to take on connotations of beauty and fashion, but the alluring mystical roots of the word remained—and still do to this day.[7]

There is a popular myth that in 1770 England when glamour was considered witchcraft, Parliament went so far as to outlaw lipstick, heels, and perfumes. They said these had the power to manipulate men into marriage. While there's no evidence that such a law passed, the morality behind the legend is historically accurate.[8] Even today, too many women know what it's like to have a toxic partner neg you for wearing too much makeup. And, frankly, compared to what men, trans people, and gender nonconforming folks deal with while trying to express themselves, cis women have it comparatively easy on the glamour front.

While today, all pretty guys, girls, and theys of the world may feel like a lot of apologizing is needed regarding a personal decision to get lip filler or rock a high-maintenance beauty routine, especially for anyone who isn't femme, that wasn't always the case. For instance, according to *Pretty Boys: Legendary Icons Who Redefined Beauty and How to Glow Up, Too*, Cyrus the Great, the ruler of the Persian Empire, considered glamour crucial to "excel his subjects but also cast a sort of spell over them." As one historian writes, "A man did not become king because he was handsome, it was because of his position as king that he was automatically designated as handsome." See? It's all about that royal swagger. But Cyrus the Great wasn't the only one allowed to be beautiful. King Cyrus expected all of his staff and royal counsel to look the part and ensured that they had glam squads to see to it.[9]

Cyrus the Great is only one diamond in a crown full of jewels of inclusive glamour history. From a Eurocentric perspective, the French Revolution somewhat marks the end of the over-the-top looks. Society-driven Victorians pinched their cheeks to make them rosy as a way to side-step sinful makeup while still getting the desired effect. (Just use the rouge, idiots!) Those days, they thought that a clean, godly life produced beauty, and sin made one ugly. Colonization spread the Puritanical message that makeup was naughty—and again, especially for men. But, for the record, countries such as South Korea have always embraced beauty as a natural desire and encouraged people of all genders to practice elaborate skin care routines. It's just part of living. Today, largely thanks to queer kids on social media, the use of beauty products and body modifications is becoming more normalized and inclusive in the United States—with a bit of help from K-pop artists such as BTS.

There is no one singular origin of glamour. Even when Victorians and conservatives would prefer otherwise, it has always existed. For example, the legendary Marie Laveau of New Orleans was both a beauty queen and Voodoo queen. Legend states that she initially became a hairdresser for money, as hairdressing was a popular alternative to household labor for Black women.

But because there's not much evidence of her beauty business, many historians assume it was simply a cover to get inside elite and white clients' houses to practice Voodoo. In an era when slavery still existed, Laveau had already developed an interracial clientele. We'll never know what happened inside those houses, but the most reasonable answer is that beauty and spell services likely overlapped. Wouldn't you rather have a hairdresser who knows how to dispose of hair clippings properly and whip up a love spell as part of styling services?

While Laveau's house, located at 1020 St. Ann Street, remains a famous New Orleans tour destination, easy access to Black hair products remains a problem. This was painfully illustrated after Hurricane Katrina in New Orleans in 2005 when the Red Cross handed out hair care for white people to the evacuees just wanting to feel human again.[10]

There may be no laws against lipstick. However, according to the Human Rights Campaign,[11] more than 250 anti-LGBTQ bills were introduced in state legislatures in 2021, including at least thirty-five that would prohibit transgender youth from accessing age-appropriate gender-affirming medical care. Glamour isn't just lipstick. It's the right to live on the outside in accordance with how you feel on the inside. As glamour witches, it is your solemn duty to fight for the rights of others to do just that.

And to ensure that you know your couture should a preppy Becky start a fight with you about a proudly hairy man's right to wear fishnets while at the club, let's have a brief fashion recap of the last century.

Glamour in History

Knowledge is power, so learn your history, babe. Stepping into another era can help you age gracefully (more on that to come) or invoke a certain mood or feel. Think of understanding these other eras as calling upon the ancestors. Different periods in history paid attention to different parts of the body. For instance, if you're flat-chested and leggy, you may enjoy the boyish short dresses of the 1920s—along with the Prohibition parties. If you've discovered how kinky housewife role-play could be, Christian Dior's "New Look" and the 1950s might be your muse. We live in the future, so you can play around as much as you want. Besides, you're all already invoking the 1990s with that goth makeup and navel piercing. Let's see what else you can do.

1900–1909

The Edwardians loved their junk. Booty, hips, and tits were in, all squeezed into an S shape with the help of the corset. Of course, the problematic—but still glam!—corset will continue to make appearances throughout history; however, this is the last decade when it was required. And as we know, any form of body modification is only enjoyable if you choose to wield it. Oh, and the corsets were made with whalebones! Poor whales, from blubber to bone we wreaked havoc on their kind.

The first few fashion designers, such as Jeanne Lanvin, were becoming famous, and *Vogue* went to print on December 17, 1892 (she's a Sag). Early coverage included advice for the widow: a black crepe veil worn over the face for six months and back from the face for twelve months to two years—or longer if one wishes. At the time, the world looked to Paris for fashion, and racecourses (Longchamp) were the center stage for style—not runways.

1910–19

Society no longer required the corset, but the bizarre hobble skirt was in. It took the cinching away from the waist and moved it to the ankles, but people certainly wore it, with tentlike tunics on top. Frankly, the divine female form deserves better. And (gasp) women showed their ankles! *Vogue* wondered if Paris had "overreached herself" and everyone clutched their pearls, while men got boners. Women were allowed to, like, drive sometimes, so sportswear was in. So was Orientalism. What we'd probably call cultural appropriation today was high fashion. Jeanne Paquin started the first fashion shows, and catwalks began giving horses and racetracks a run for their money. And then, in 1914, World War I broke out.

The big takeaway from this decade is how war impacts fashion. Darker colors were in because people had so many fucking funerals to attend. Opulence declined, and people opted for jewelry made of glass instead of diamonds. Women chose bobbed hair over long tresses because it makes working in hot factories easier. The Great War ended in 1918, and the celebrations would spill over into the next decade. Beauty history was also made in 1918. Black investors formed the Kashmir Chemical Co., producing Queen Nile cosmetics, one of the first brands created for Black people by Black people.

1920–29

The exaggerated curvy figure was out, and the boyish flapper look was in. Dresses became shorter with straight lines, and women could finally sit—and dance. People put on their party clothes to celebrate the end of the war, but then the government did something superlame and outlawed alcohol in 1920. You know what happens next because banning alcohol doesn't work. People partied harder. Outfits got sluttier. Ladies had to kick up their heels to do the Charleston, after all!

The accessories were simply fabulous. Art deco was a significant influence. Think fans to bat while flirting, giant feathers stuck in hats, strands of pearls, and elegant cigarette holders. It was unheard of to see a woman smoke in public years ago! The 1920s were progressive for the time, and androgynous looks were in. *Vogue* even wrote about what to wear for your second marriage! Problematic—she was a bit of a Nazi—Coco Chanel opened her first London store, and everyone went nuts for her straight-cut suit. In 1925, the trendiest makeup look on the block was called "pallor mortis," which means paleness of death. The style features white skin, scarlet lips, and lined eyes with plenty of mascara.

1930–39

Alas, the Great Depression. Wall Street, am I right? First, the government kept all the silk for war materials, and as a result, designers were forced to use new, cheaper materials such as rayon and synthetic nylon for stockings. Then the government also took the nylon, leaving stocking-wearers only cotton and rayon. When nylon reappeared, there were riots at department stores around the United States—dubbed the "nylon riots" naturally. The zipper was also invented. Because clothing became more affordable, more people had access to fashion, making this an exciting decade despite the crash.

Shoulders were popular and all over the place. There were square shoulders, high shoulders, boxy shoulders, and sleek shoulders. Women in factories began wearing pants, but these articles of clothing were still taboo in mainstream society. Hollywood's influence continued. *Tarzan, the Ape Man,* came out in 1932 and popularized animal prints. The 1930s were monumental for the United States, despite how badly Wall Street had fucked up. Fred Astaire and Joan Crawford were among the first stars to grab attention for their style. The—also problematic, like most films from this era—1939 *Gone with the Wind* brought back neo-Victorian looks. When World War II began in 1939, people welcomed doomsday chic by carrying around respiratory pouches in case of a poison gas attack.

1940–49

The world was at war again. Bombs fell on London and Paris. As stockings were rationed once again, fashion became a symbol of hope. Women painted back seams on their legs like an old-fashioned tattoo. The iconic "Fashion Is Indestructible" photo shoot featured a woman in a neat suit walking amid the rubble in London. In place of hats, women wore snoods and scarves. All the fabric was going to war along with the men! Women took to the factories, and Rosie the Riveter rocked a bandana. Uniforms were the uniform of the first half of the decade. Swimwear companies invented the bikini as they had to use 10 percent less fabric. Violence breeds sluttiness.

World War II ended, and then . . . In 1947 Christian Dior launched his New Look, and everything changed. Femininity was back. His collection featured wide skirts, cinched waists, and slim shoulders. Gone were the boyish looks of the 1920s.

1950–59

Oh, the glamour of the 1950s! Did you know this was when false eyelashes became oh so popular? You simply had to be put together. Poise and posture were important, and fashion became accessible and marketed to all ages. The industry realized that it could make money off teenagers, and Gloria

Swanson starred in *Sunset Boulevard* at fifty-one years old. All ages looked fabulous in fifties fashion. Dior's New Look was still all the rage, but he was now making fitted skirts in addition to flouncy full ones. Givenchy launched in 1952, and Audrey Hepburn was his muse. She wasn't alone. America rose in the fashion world's eyes as television and Hollywood continued to be a significant source of fashion inspiration. The term "sweater girl" describes such Hollywood actresses, who wore tight, formfitting sweaters that emphasized their fantastic boobs.

The 1950s followed pretty strict gender roles. Corsets came back, as did the "cathedral bra," the pointed-tits look that icons such as Marilyn Monroe and Lana Turner would popularize in the fifties. Men wore double-breasted, broad-shouldered suits. This era was postwar celebratory yet restrictive and conservative, emphasizing the heteronormative nuclear family.

1960–69

Makeup and style became less about the woman and more about the baby girl in this decade. Skinny minis like supermodel Jean Shrimpton covered magazines in white collars and massive bows. It was all about legs, legs, legs, as people paired miniskirts with baby shoes. Supermodel Twiggy perpetuated this, as did Andy Warhol's muse Edie Sedgwick, who also helped shift the erotic focal point to the legs. All hail the "angel dress," a micromini with a flared skirt and long, wide trumpet sleeves, best paired with patterned tights.

There was also another new fashion icon: Jackie Kennedy. She was gorgeous, classy as pearls, and, in 1963, wore a pink Chanel suit covered in her husband's blood. Men took on a more significant part of the fashion game, embracing proper suits. The musical *Hair* became a smash hit showcasing hippie fashion. Black women rocked their Afros, and white women tried to imitate them. Fashion shoots included models of more than one race for the first time. Nigerian jewelry made its way into the 1969 September *Vogue*, and just a decade after the prim and proper 1950s, rock stars such as Jimi Hendrix made it impossible to shock anyone. Prints were psychedelic. Jeans grew bell-bottoms, and men's hair was longer than women's. Women wore pants, and it wasn't even weird anymore! Lipstick became paler. Cute baby pinks replaced the glamorous dark red. Second-wave feminism was taking hold, and the new look became "The Single Girl." She wore minidresses with psychedelic prints, listened to the Beatles, and strutted to work. Yes, she had a job!

The Space Race was on, and fashion was inspired. There were plastic, PVC, and leather dresses, all short and paired with go-go boots. The Stonewall Riots occurred in 1969, making it impossible to ignore the queer community, and certainly not Marsha P. Johnson's iconic flower crowns.

1970–79

You could tell the 1970s were going to be lit because *Vogue's* first directive of the decade read: "You are one of a kind, unique in fashion. Forget rules—you make them, you break them." David Bowie's *Space Oddity* came out in 1969, and by the seventies, glam rock had arrived. Skirts were short enough to easily fuck in—ideally in the bathroom of Studio 54—and cocaine was part of a well-rounded diet. Music and fashion finally consummate their relationship, and A-list designers went to work for Mick Jagger.

Despite the plethora of sequins and disco balls, this decade also brought minimalism thanks to designers such as Halston. The rise of disco required danceable fabric. It was an era of little clothing and lots of skin, and as a result, people paid more attention to the body. Vivienne Westwood opened her shop SEX on London's King's Road with her partner Malcolm McClare, who "mismanaged" the Sex Pistols. Punk was here, and the kids shoved safety pins through their ears, sewed spikes on their jackets, and dyed their hair green.

Beauty went neon. In 1971, Maybelline introduced Great Lash mascara in its hot pink and slime green tube, which is still available today—and what I wear; after all, you can get it at the drugstore for a fraction of what designer mascaras cost, and it works wonderfully. CoverGirl introduced "shiny shadows," creamy, shimmery eyeshadows in pastel purple, blue, and green. Pastels were everywhere! Following the space trend, Max Factor released its first transparent lipstick in 1972 and called it "Earthlings." Hair was worn long and straight with a middle part.

There was also a rise in casual chic despite the glitz and glam. The T-shirt was no longer an undergarment but something worn every day and adorned with slogans. Accessories included gold jewelry, boas, boots for every occasion, and the mood ring. By the way, if you're wondering if mood cock rings exist today, the answer is yes. Speaking of, the seventies let men dress flamboyantly, too. Victorian neck ruffles and satin shirts dominated the trend dubbed the Peacock Revolution.

The Black Panthers and other Black power groups popularized military fashion, peaked caps, and Afros—with a custom comb with a fist on the handle.

Traditional African clothing and colors such as red, yellow, and green made a statement. Due to social inequality, urban Black youth wore whatever clothing they could get, which would inspire the baggy pants of the 1980s hip-hop trends that white folks would inevitably copy.

1980–89

Only one person can introduce us to the 1980s: the mighty glamour witch Princess Diana. Her baby face and model 5'10" frame became the most photographed combo in the world. And what is that coquettish and devilish look in her eye? It's glamour, honey, glamour! Vivienne Westwood got bored of punk and started dressing people up like pirates. The problematic Chanel hired the even more problematic Karl Lagerfeld. America's sweetheart became Nancy Reagan, but I really can't type that much more about her without becoming sick to my stomach. (The racist War on Drugs! The denial and homophobic joking about the AIDS crisis! Mrs. Reagan was *not* a glamour witch.) Across the pond, Margaret Thatcher matched her hair and suits to the severity of her politics.

A lovely trend began known as "The New Romantics," which meant stunning androgynous styles such as seen on Boy George, described as "shock romance," and born out of glam rock. Tokyo was wearing modern looks in all black, which Americans took on. Alaïa put models in slutty little dresses that cinched the body like a corset. Designers also started putting pre-woke slogans on their expensive T-shirts. For instance, Katharine Hamnett saved the Earth with her "Stop Acid Rain" shirt. Kidding—but come on. Thankfully, Versace came along and gave the people what they wanted: glamour, glitz, opulent fashion.

Women were working the stock exchange and wearing the power suit! Shoulder pads! Short skirts! Get it, bitch. Soap operas started to influence fashion almost as much as Princess Diana did. Makeup of the 1980s was . . . well, you know. A 1986 Aziza eyeshadow ad said it best: "Not for the meek."

1990–99

The 1990s were the era of the supermodel. The new royalty were Linda Evangelista, Naomi Campbell, Christy Turlington, and Cindy Crawford. And they wouldn't get out of bed for less than $10,000 a day. Princess Diana was divorced, free, on the cover of *Vogue* in a black turtleneck, and out and about in short dresses and high heels. Alexander McQueen entered the scene, and people rioted to get into his shows. Grunge fashion was in. Skinny mini Kate Moss appeared in *Vogue*'s first grunge shoot and infamous Calvin Klein ads that prompted people to graffiti them with the words "feed me"—still a form of body shaming, in my opinion. Let Kate live!

Elizabeth Hurley iconically attended the premiere of *Four Weddings and a Funeral* in a black Versace dress held together with safety pins. Logos were in. You had to have the silver and black Prada triangle and the gold Gucci horsebit. In 1997 Princess Diana was tragically taken from the world, and the world

mourned. The clothing and jewelry found at the time of Diana's death included a pair of slip-on Gianni Versace black satin stilettos, a Giorgio Armani jacket, and six white pearls.

Body modifications such as tattoos and piercings, previously only seen in subcultures, went mainstream. In 1993 the MTV Video Music Awards Music Video of the Year "Cryin'" by Aerosmith featured Alicia Silverstone getting pierced. And the neon, oh, the neon! Much like with the grunge look, exercise clothing was acceptable in public even though it was meant to be worn when one needed to shower. And as if Bill Clinton didn't tip you off, the nineties were kinky, although problematic. The schoolgirl look was demonstrated in films such as *Clueless* and *The Craft*. Britney Spears would officially own it with the 1998 video for "Baby One More Time." While it is Britney's right to own that schoolgirl look, the way the media handled the icon is, well, iconically fucked up.

Hip-hop was mainstream and so was its fashion. Sportswear, baggy pants, and tracksuits became co-opted while conservatives continued to furrow their brows at the rising influence of Black culture. The goth movement, which began in the eighties, hit its crescendo. All black, Victorian aesthetics, frilly poet shirts, and fetish clothing were batty and beloved. Goth makeup looks caught on with the general public, such as dark, smudged lips and heavy eyeliner. The coolest haircut was "the Rachel"—although people wore all sorts of shit during the nineties, like the zigzag part, scrunchies, and sidebangs. Nails become talons as colorful acrylics were introduced.

Science met beauty, so lipsticks contained SPF and moisturizer; mascara formulas claimed to lengthen, add volume, and even promote eyelash growth. Skin care products added an array of vitamins to help prevent "premature aging." Remember: a proper skin care regime is essential, but if you want to zap away lines and wrinkles, you need Botox, baby—which only became FDA-approved for cosmetic use in 2002. Unfortunately, while androgyny became more mainstream, it was still painfully easier for a woman to dress in menswear than for a man to put on a dress.

Gender

Being transgender is not just a medical transition; it's discovering who you are, living your life authentically, loving yourself, and spreading that love towards other people and accepting one another no matter the difference.

—Jazz Jennings[12]

What a time to be alive, glamour witches. We're in a gender revolution, and there's no going back. Transgender icons such as Elliot Page and Laverne Cox continuously use their fame to inspire and break boundaries. However, while Hollywood is finally starting to admit that trans roles should go to trans actors, unfortunately, modern-day society still has a long way to go. At the time of publishing, the Human Rights Campaign reports that the year 2021 saw at least thirty-four transgender or gender nonconforming people fatally shot or killed by other violent means. Cox herself was the victim of a hate crime in Los Angeles in 2020. "It's not safe if you're a trans person," she said in an Instagram video posted shortly after the incident.

Gender exists for social organization and is different than biological sex. However, prescribed gender roles are relatively recent. We view the Enlightenment as a time of, well, enlightenment. But in *Making Sex: Body and Gender from the Greeks to Freud*, author Thomas Laqueur[13] proposes that until the Enlightenment, society considered men and women as physical equals, so it was no biggie if a man wanted to wear makeup. During what historians call "The Great Male Renunciation," the British became very into gender binaries, and boys weren't supposed to be pretty. American psychologist Dr. John Carl Flügel, who coined the term, states that men "abandoned their claim to be considered beautiful" and refocused simply on being useful. How drab!

According to *Pretty Boys: Legendary Icons Who Redefined Beauty and How to Glow Up, Too*,[14] while the United States seems insistent on enforcing binary gender roles, in other cultures it's no big deal. It's not only not a big deal, but nonbinary folks are often rightfully considered magickal. For example, Oaxaca, Mexico, has a third gender called *muxes*. They live together in a region called Istmo de Tehuantepec. Legend states that a saint, Vicente Ferrer, came through and sprinkled seeds from three bags: male, female, and a mixed bag. The mixed bag became the muxes, who in their language of Zapotec use gender-neutral pronouns.

In Hawaii, the gender-neutral *mahu* are considered sacred beings and often help teach communities about the importance of balancing the masculine and feminine. However, ever since Hawaii became part of the United States, naturally, we've been dicks about it. So they face persecution today.

Everyone's heard of Thailand's *kathoey* or the more derogatory "ladyboys." But, while Western media likes to focus on the fetishization of the kathoey, Thailand has remained somewhat free from colonization, so they do have a more accepting gender understanding as a country. Unfortunately, however, sex tourists aren't always nice, and as a result, even Thailand hasn't been able to protect them from exploitation and violence. Additional examples include the two-spirit people from Indigenous North American tribes, the *hijras* of India, and the *khawaja sira* of Pakistan.

Of course, there is persecution for every example in which trans and gender nonconforming folks are celebrated. It's certainly not just the United States that feels threatened by breaks in the gender binary. In Saudi Arabia, "men behaving as women" can receive 100 lashes or banishment. And, of course, under their interpretation of Sharia law, consensual homosexuality can get you the death penalty.[15]

It's crucial to understand that not every trans or nonbinary person can safely come out. Even in the United States, it can still get you killed. Gender nonconforming folks are not only magickal, but they're brave. If you can express yourself, don't take it for granted. Men are allowed to be feminine, adore ballet, and love crying through fake eyelashes. Women are allowed to grow body hair and know how to cut firewood. Everyone is allowed to reject the gender binary entirely. As the Backstreet Boys should have sung—I don't care who you are, where you're from, don't care what you did, as long as you respect others. All glamour witches should be up to date with modern-day pronouns and gender terminology, so take a look at this handy cheat sheet.

Common pronouns include:

He/Him/His/Himself

She/Her/Hers/Herself

They/Them/Theirs/Themself

Fae/Faer/Faers/Faerself (yes, these pronouns are fae and fairy inspired)

Ze/Zir/Zem/Zeir (sometimes used as xe)

Name (Some people prefer their name to any pronouns at all!)

Remember, people can also have multiple pronouns. All you have to do is ask. And here are some gender terms everyone should know:[16]

Cisgender: Cisgender folks are those whose gender identity matches those associated with their sex assigned at birth.

Gender Binary: The gender binary is a system that constructs gender into solely two categories of male or female. In the gender binary, society expects one's gender identity and expression to align with the sex assigned at birth.

Gender Dysphoria: This refers to the life-disrupting distress occurring when one's gender does not match the sex assigned at birth, but you are expected to shut up and play by the rules.

Gender Expression: Gender expression refers to external appearance. It's how one utilizes glamour to express oneself through clothing, makeup, behavior, and more.

Gender Fluid: Someone who is genderfluid has a changeable rather than distinct fixed gender.

Gender Nonconforming, or GNC: This is an umbrella term for those whose gender does not fit into the binary.

Genderqueer: People who are genderqueer reject static gender binaries. It's also an umbrella term and encompasses identities such as gender fluid and nonbinary.

Intersex: Intersex folks are born with reproductive or sexual anatomy that doesn't fit neatly into the boxes of female or male. This can include a large clitoris that presents more like a penis, a lack of a vaginal opening, a small penis that looks more like a clit, or differences in chromosomes or hormone responses. While, historically, doctors often designate sex at birth and even perform surgeries, increasingly—and finally—intersex people are being allowed to make their own medical decisions.

Nonbinary: The term describes those who do not identify as solely male or female. They may identify as both, neither, or somewhere in between. One can also identify as both trans and nonbinary.

Transgender or trans: This term refers to people whose gender identity does not match their biological sex assigned at birth.

Orientation

I'm like, so gay, dude.
—Kristen Stewart[17]

Maud Galt was a lesbian accused of witchcraft in seventeenth-century Scotland. Knowing how much trouble she'd get into if people found out about her orientation, she protected her sexual identity by marrying a man, John Dickie. But sexual orientation isn't something that likes to hide. Galt had a relationship with one of her servants, a woman named Agnes Mitchell. The records are unclear on precisely what transpired and how, but Mitchell filed a complaint against Galt, stating that she was "abusing ane of hir servants with ane peis of clay formed lyk the secreit member of ane man." Yes, that means a dildo.

"Women throughout Europe had been burned for possession of such prostheses, especially when used while cross-dressed. This specifically represents the idea of 'counterfeiting the office of husband', a type of deception in which the woman threatened to replace the man, not only economically but sexually," writes one historian.[18] Not only did Galt's actions display lesbianism, but they trespassed on gender roles, and perhaps most offensively, threatened masculinity. If Galt's actions were nonconsensual, that's not cool, but what we do know from this incident is that apparently, some cishet men have always been threatened by sex toys. While it's unclear from historical records whether Galt was charged, authorities investigated the case as witchcraft.

Dildos are a form of glamour. They prove that anyone can have a dick, whether it's modern medical-grade silicone or "ane peis of clay." Dildos allow people with vaginas to enjoy penetrative sex with one another, and they allow folks to express their gender identity. Unfortunately, they also continue to elicit shock today.

In 2015, pansexual pop star Miley Cyrus wore a strap-on during her "Dead Petz" tour with the Flaming Lips.[19] "Miley Cyrus Takes Shocking To Next Level With Strap-On Dildo," read one of many pearl-clutching headlines on the fashion statement.[20] While Cyrus is hardly an accurate representation for most LGBTQIA+ folks, the public's reaction shows just how scary queer chicks—and especially queer chicks with dicks—continue to be. But while such outward expressions of queerness in a heteronormative society cause some to clutch their pearls, glamour simply wouldn't be glamour without the queers. Examples include Billy Porter's iconic 2020 Grammy Awards Baja East blue crystal-encrusted ensemble featuring a Sarah Sokol hat designed by Porter himself. The hat was motorized with crystal curtains, which he could draw back when he was tired of looking at the paparazzi. And who can forget Janelle Monáe's multi-hat Christian Siriano look at the 2019 Met Gala, which featured an opulent eye covering her breast that she could make wink. We truly owe the LGBTQIA+ community for glamour's greatest moments.

Perhaps the most influential of them is RuPaul, who brought drag mainstream. After escaping a tumultuous childhood and making his way to New York City, RuPaul—yes, that's his real name—found a home in the club kids scene after landing a gig as a go-go dancer at the famed Pyramid Club. He may have been a New York City celebrity, but RuPaul contemplated suicide. It was the 1980s; what could the future hold for a 6'4" (7' with heels) drag queen? But after landing a smash hit with his 1992 track "Supermodel (You Better Work)" and becoming MAC Cosmetics' first drag spokesperson, he landed his VH1 *RuPaul Show*. This would lead to *RuPaul's Drag Race*, which is now a household name and launched careers for a plethora of other worthy drag queens. After all, drag queens are the greatest glamour witches, and later in this book, you'll learn how to form your own drag identity. But first, let's make sure that you're up to date on queer terminology.[21]

Here are some sexual orientation terms that you should know:[22]

Asexual: Asexual, often abbreviated as ace, refers to someone with little or no sexual attraction to others. Like so many orientations, it exists on a spectrum and can be subject to change.

Bisexual: Bisexuals are attracted to their own gender as well as others. Contrary to harmful misconception, bisexuals do not date exclusively on the gender binary.

Gay: Gay people are sexually and romantically attracted to their same gender. Any and all genders can identify as gay.

Lesbian: Historically, lesbian refers to women who are attracted to and date other women. Today, both women and gender nonconforming folks use the term.

LGBTQIA+: This is an acronym for "lesbian, gay, bisexual, transgender, queer, intersex, and asexual plus." People in the community sometimes refer to it as the "alphabet soup," and it is sometimes lengthened to LGBTQQIP2SAA (lesbian, gay, bisexual, transgender, questioning, queer, intersex, pansexual, two-spirit, androgynous and asexual). It may evolve further as our understanding of orientation develops and becomes more inclusive.

Pansexual: Like bisexuality, people who are pansexual are attracted to their own gender and others. Pansexuality can be described as attraction to folks based on other factors regardless of their gender.

Queer: Once upon a time, queer was a slur. Today, it's embraced by LGBTQIA+ folks to describe not only a nonheterosexual orientation, but to curate and create community.

Questioning: Are you unsure of your sexual orientation? That's OK! Welcome to the family. Questioning refers to people who are exploring their orientation and/or gender.

2

MAGICK SCHOOL

It's hard to talk about magick school without mentioning that J. K. Rowling is a mean bully. However, if we let her ruin Hogwarts, the TERFs win. Anyone who makes transphobic comments at Glamour Witch Finishing School will be immediately expelled and hexed with bad brows and incurable foot odor for life.

If you've ever chosen a gold blazer to slay a job interview or dyed your hair poison green to remind people to stay the fuck away, you might already be doing glamour magick. Oh, and that vanity filled with perfumes and skin creams? Yeah, you might even already have an altar.

But to graduate to being a total witch, let's review some pillars of witchcraft. If you understand astrology, you know that a new moon in Scorpio is the perfect day for a makeover, but don't you dare do anything drastic to your appearance during Venus retrograde. With even a basic witch understanding of tarot, you know to go ahead and start dancing to "Single Ladies" if you pull a Nine of Pentacles because money is coming, honey. Let's get started.

Color Magick

Both the fashion industry and the magickal community have been using color magick since before Jesus existed. And when you learn how to overlay the two, you're doing glamour magick.

Just as you might put on a pink Kate Spade sweater to show your partner's parents that you're a good girl, if you want to inject your romantic relationship with nurturing, sweet love, a pink candle is just the thing. Rose quartz is the go-to crystal for attracting love. It's also frequently found in beauty products such as skin rollers and even nail polishes.

However, if you're dealing with creative blocks and in need of a self-esteem boost, work with purple. Queen Elizabeth I banned anyone except close members of the royal family from wearing purple. And when Lil Nas X showed up at the 2021 MTV Video Music Awards wearing a lavender Versace pantsuit with a jewel-encrusted jacket, a long train, and an asymmetrical off-the-shoulder silhouette, complete with matching shoes, he was total royalty.

Once you understand what different colors signify, you can not only integrate them into spellwork but also use clothing and makeup more intentionally.

Red

Red is the color of hot sex and often used in love spells. And science supports this. The "red dress effect" demonstrates that men rate women wearing red clothing more interested in sex, suggesting that humans associate the color with fertility. It's why red is the first color on record to be turned into lipstick and why you can't go wrong wearing red on a first date. When Alicia Silverstone shouted, "this is an Alaia!" while getting mugged wearing the designer's dress in *Clueless*, she was all red energy.

Cher Horowitz aside, the devil is also often depicted in red to illustrate the fiery, animalistic, and perhaps evil nature of passion. Mars, which rules fucking and fighting, is the color red. Red garnet is a helpful crystal to work with to attract erotic love.

A red candle is ideal for a romantic candle spell rooted in passion. And for extra oomph, anoint the candle in blood—any blood will do, but you don't want to self-harm, so use period blood if you menstruate. Red is the color of blood, after all. It's also associated with so-called sinful pleasure, which is probably why popular depictions paint the devil red. Its uses span from the red-bottomed shoes of Christian Louboutin to the REDress project, created by artist Jaime Black. This art installation honors the potentially thousands of Native American women who go missing or are murdered each year.

Orange

Orange is the eccentric color that is the hair of Ziggy Stardust—aka the problem rock star from space embodied by David Bowie. It's also associated with creativity, as demonstrated by fellow glamour witch Frank Ocean's iconic album *Channel Orange*. So it makes sense that orange candles are great for spells when you want to break through creative blocks. Likewise, the orange-streaked crystal citrine is fabulous for manifesting money.

Orange was a color heavily used in the psychedelic 1960s and '70s. It's sure to bring you attention, as demonstrated with its use on caution signs and not-so-sexy traffic crossing vests and life jackets. It's a color of transformation and uniqueness—think of Milla Jovovich as Leeloo in the movie *The 5th Element*.

Monet famously used the color orange, showing that the color can range from the sunrises of impressionists to prison jumpsuits. Orange brings attention, whether that's used for good or evil.

Yellow

Yellow is the color of sunshine and happiness. So when you see a yellow background in a tarot card (citing the Rider-Waite-Smith tarot deck), it's a sign of abundance and prosperity—opt for yellow candles when you want to bring more joy into your life. Citrine, as mentioned above—which has shades of yellow in addition to orange—is another witchy tool to attract abundance.

Because yellow is associated with the sun, it's a close cousin to gold. Here's a fun fact: Satanist Anton Szandor LaVey wrote against wearing gold because he associated it with Christian sun gods. Instead, he encouraged Satanists to wear silver. Judas is portrayed as wearing yellow, which may be responsible for some of the cowardly associations with the color, such as the term *yellow-bellied*. Yellow is a color of contradictions. We see it in high fashion, such as RiRi's Guo Pei gown and cape at the 2015's "China: Through the Looking Glass" Met Gala and Beyoncé's mustard Roberto Cavalli gown accessorized with a baseball bat in Lemonade's "Hold Up" music video. And we can't forget Belle in *Beauty and the Beast*. However, polls show that it is people's least favorite color.

Green

Green is the color of health, nature, and money, honey. So, if you need a candle for a money spell, opt for green. Green jade is an excellent stone to keep on hand for attracting prosperity. Green's associations of abundance may stem from the fact that it's the color of the chlorophyll essential in photosynthesis—the process that allows plants to absorb energy from light.

Recently, green has become the color of environmentalism—"going green"—but in the Middle Ages, bankers wore green. It's the color of frogs, emeralds, absinthe, and envy. It has some rather outrageous connotations as well. In Victorian England, green was associated with homosexuality. Bela Lugosi wore green when he played Dracula. So, whether you're a nature freak, into the decay of vampires, or simply gay, green is the color for you! Just don't wear anything dyed with Scheele's Green, popular in the nineteenth century. Its main ingredient was arsenic, which made gowns deadly.

We see green more vividly than other colors because it exists at the middle of the spectrum, a wavelength our perception is best at detecting. It's used in hospitals and even prisons because, apparently, it can calm you down. It's considered holy in Islam.

Blue

The color of the ocean, blue represents the tranquility found in a calm sea. Yet, despite its calming reputation, it is also associated with sadness, such as in the expression "got the blues." Picasso's morbidly beautiful blue period began shortly after he discovered a close friend's suicide.

Despite some sad connotations, we usually use blue for spells to invoke peace and tranquility within witchcraft. After all, inner peace isn't possible until you make friends with your demons. So, if you're looking for a blue crystal, lapis lazuli not only helps with protection but also enhances psychic powers and intuition. Blue is also an excellent candle color selection for a house-blessing spell.

Blue flowers exist, but only through human manipulation. Blue is the perfect hair color for a hot tattooed gamer, although no one pulls off blue hair like BTS's V. Blue is also blue jeans and Bruce Springsteen, Lana Del Rey, the Democratic Party, and a token worn by brides. It's associated with baby boys, but we know that gender reveal parties are for old-fashioned losers.

The Virgin Mary wore a blue robe, and it's a color of authority as found in police uniforms. Blue-collar means working-class, but blue stockings refer to an organization of mid-eighteenth-century women who placed conversation over fashion. As a result, the term now has a feminist association—but you can like both fashion and good conversation.

Purple

Purple is a royal and creative color. Tyrian purple is a dye first created in 1200 BCE by the Phoenicians. The Greeks and Romans also used it. It is associated with the wealthy upper class, as it was then costly to make. And what was the secret ingredient? Snail mucus.

Later on, Queen Victoria wore a purple dress and made it one of the most fashionable colors of her era. Purple continues to be associated with royalty today. In the nineteenth century, purple became a color of demi-mourning, worn by widows after their black phase but before their return to typical dress.

It's the color used in psychedelic culture and songs like Jimi Hendrix's "Purple Haze." Hendrix is far from the only musical artist to invoke the color; just take a listen to Prince's "Purple Rain." Purple candles work wonders to summon creativity or add a boost of royal fabulousness into your life. The purple crystal amethyst is a gorgeous healing stone that can also boost your psychic power.

Purple is the color of the politically split state and, of course, most importantly, bisexuality, as our pride flag displays. Activist Michael Page created the bisexual flag, and it was unveiled at BiCafe's first Anniversary Party on December 5, 1998 (they're a Sag). "The intent and purpose of the flag is to maximize bisexual pride and visibility," Page said.[23] The flag's colors are a combination of magenta, lavender, and royal blue. The bi flag is inspired by the biangles—two overlapping triangles, one blue and one pink, which is another, not quite as famous, bi symbol.

Pink

Pink is historically associated with girls, but according to *Smithsonian Magazine*, all children, regardless of gender, wore white dresses for a long time.[24] There is a famous picture of Franklin D. Roosevelt looking beautiful as a baby in a dress in 1884. He even had long hair to match. Before then, at times pink was even marketed more toward boys than girls. For example, a June 1918 article from the trade publication *Earnshaw's Infants' Department* said, "The generally accepted rule is pink for the boys, and blue for the girls. The reason is that pink, being a more decided and stronger color, is more suitable for the boy, while blue, which is more delicate and dainty, is prettier for the girl." But by the 1940s, thanks to manufacturers, retailers, and marketing, blue was for boys and pink was for girls. That is ridiculous. Machine Gun Kelly's 2020 MTV Video Music Awards monochrome Barbie pink Berluti outfit proves that the color makes anyone look like a god. Gender is over—you can don any color you like.

Today we associate pink with the divine feminine (which we all contain regardless of gender), self-love, and friendship. Light pink, or blush, is a popular alternative wedding dress color to white—but extra goth points for the brides who wear black.

Use pink candles for spells to inject tender sweetness into the relationship. Rose quartz is a stone of sweet love. And let's be honest, all genitals usually have a tinge of the color! Pink is also associated with literal sweets, such as cupcakes, and as a bonus it's an insult to fake communists—pink being a watered-down version of red.

Your Glamour Altar

Typically, we think of an altar as a table of sorts. The witch in question will decorate it with a grimoire or spellbook, crystals, tarot cards, and perhaps a candle spell. There may also likely be odd items such as a preserved snake or scorpion, a handful of their lover's hair, and toenail clippings of an enemy—if one is very lucky.

A vanity is just another kind of altar. Your makeup brushes and curling iron are magickal tools. Face oils and lotions are potions. As anyone who uses glitter both in their eyeshadow and in their candle magick can attest, you may notice the overlap in the Venn diagram of standard witch altar and vanity. Getting your glam on is a ritual that is best done in a gorgeous robe. When you put on your makeup, you're casting a spell—just like the Puritans suspected.

As we move through this book, I also want you to start thinking of your body as an altar—a beautiful living altar to Venus, the goddess of love, beauty, and abundance. Your shoes, the way you walk, your posture—it all can become

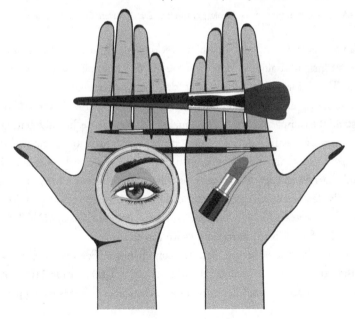

a dance of intimidating beauty. Your clothing is your armor. Your makeup is your war paint. Your body, your choice: you can decorate your altar however you desire. Some days what your body needs may be sweatpants and greasy hair. Other days require an outfit and makeup look that could kill a bitch and steal her lover. But you should never feel guilty for putting time and effort into your presentation. Life is too short to spend it looking drab.

Astrology Glamour

Astrology empowers and adds to our aesthetic. Whether we are channeling one of our planetary placements, or harnessing the mythology of a planet (Taurus in field of flowers or the Gemini twins in matching outfits, Jupiter's decadence or Saturn's polished and tailored presence), astrology inspires our imaginations and suggests a starting point with which to imagine a look for an evening, or even an entire wardrobe!

—Annabel Gat, author of *The Astrology of Love and Sex: A Modern Compatibility Guide*[25]

What's your sign? It's actually a fabulous pickup line. Your sun sign provides a limited yet insightful glimpse into who you are. For example, Laverne Cox is a Gemini. This information tells us that she's witty, charismatic, and probably a heartbreaker. This information does not mean that we know Laverne Cox or understand the complexities of her personality and experience. Just like getting to know someone takes time and effort, understanding astrology ideally entails looking at one's entire chart. Obtain your birth time—and your crush's—to see what your full chart looks like. (Many websites will do all of the work for you.) From this, you also learn your rising sign, or the mask you wear to the world; your Venus sign, which indicates how you act in love; and so on. But your sun sign? Well, that's just enough information to start flirting with someone.

You can also use your sun sign as glamour-inspo. For instance, did you know that there are colors associated with each sign? The color for Aries is red, which is perfect for the bold fire sign. It's also the color of Aries's ruling planet,

Mars, which governs how we fuck and fight. So, whether you're an Aries, trying to relate to your Aries crush, or just looking to channel some firepower before a first date or interview, integrating astrology color magick is just one way to harness the glamour of the stars. Each sign also corresponds with an element: fire, earth, air, and water. For example, if you're a Pisces, a water sign, you'll probably enjoy baths as a health and beauty ritual. Or, if you are a stubborn earth sign looking to get in touch with your emotions, take a page from Pisces's book and practice self-love with bath magick.

In the spell section of this book, you'll notice that certain ones consider astrology regarding when to cast them. For instance, because Scorpio is the sign of sex, death, and transformation, when the moon is in Scorpio it's an excellent

time for a makeover. But mostly, astrology is just another helpful tool in your glamour witch arsenal. So keep reading to learn the basics of each sign, as well as their glamour superpowers. Because, even if you aren't a Virgo, you want to apply a winged eyeliner with Virgo precision.

Aries

Dates: March 21–April 19

Symbol: Ram

Element: Fire

Planetary ruler: Mars

Modality: Cardinal

Tarot card: The Emperor

Color: Red

Superpower: It's highly contested, but with their sexy self-assurance, Aries might be the greatest heartbreaker of the zodiac.

Beauty trick: A bold red lip can make any outfit chic. Revlon Lipstick in Fire and Ice is still iconic nearly seventy years later, and Yves Saint Laurent's reds are to die for. A swipe of red lipstick and some sunglasses are all you need to look like a celebrity walking down 5th Avenue.

Glam witch icons: Mariah Carey, Elton John, Diana Ross, Lady Gaga

Taurus

Dates: April 20–May 20

Symbol: Bull

Element: Earth

Planetary ruler: Venus

Modality: Fixed

Tarot card: The Hierophant

Color: Earth greens

Superpower: Tauruses are the ultimate pillow princesses. They always snag lovers who give the best massages.

Beauty trick: Every glamour witch must know how to prepare a charcuterie board for having friends and lovers over. Buy a vintage tray off of eBay or a cottage-core cutting board. Fill it with sliced cheese, meats, fruits (can't go wrong with grapes), and crackers. Make sure to include some hummus and gluten-free options for all the glam witches who are vegans or have gluten allergies.

Glam witch icons: Janet Jackson, Cher, Grace Jones, Dwayne "The Rock" Johnson

Gemini

Dates: May 21–June 20

Symbol: Twins

Element: Air

Planetary ruler: Mercury

Modality: Mutable

Tarot card: The Lovers

Color: Yellow

Superpower: Everyone wants to fuck a Gemini. I don't know how they get any work done while they're busy teaching the world to make love.

Beauty trick: Keep on-the-go cleansing wipes with you. Always! Use them to wipe off makeup at an unexpected sleepover or clean up after having hot messy sex in someone else's apartment.

Glam witch icons: Stevie Nicks, Prince, Angelina Jolie, Marilyn Monroe

Cancer

Dates: June 21–July 22

Symbol: Crab

Element: Water

Planetary ruler: The moon

Modality: Cardinal

Tarot card: The Chariot

Color: Silver

Superpower: Cancer's superpower is tricking you into thinking they're just cute sweetness tied up in a bow. Just wait until you feel their pinchers—these crabs break just as many hearts as Geminis.

Beauty trick: Have a signature scent, but that doesn't mean that you're 100 percent monogamous with that perfume. You can set up all your perfumes on an altar like gorgeous tiny gravestones.

Glam witch icons: Ariana Grande, Lana Del Rey, Princess Diana, Frida Kahlo

Leo

Dates: July 23–August 22

Symbol: Lion

Element: Fire

Planetary ruler: The sun

Modality: Fixed

Tarot card: Strength

Color: Gold

Superpower: No matter what they look like, Leos act like they're hot—making them desirable because confidence is everything.

Beauty trick: The truth is important to Leos. For instance, no night cream will zap away wrinkles, no matter how expensive. Topicals simply don't penetrate the skin deeply enough. If you want to reduce aging, get some Botox, and act like a lion. Give zero fucks what anyone else thinks about your decision.

Glam witch icons: Barack Obama, Madonna, Mick Jagger, Jennifer Lopez

Virgo

Dates: August 23–September 22

Symbol: Virgin

Element: Earth

Planetary ruler: Mercury

Modality: Mutable

Tarot card: The Hermit

Color: Green

Superpower: Virgos make perfection seem easy, but in reality, their success results from lots of practice, hard work, and meticulous attention to detail.

Beauty trick: You should know how to create a perfect winged eyeliner. First, get yourself a black liquid liner. Then, starting at the edge of your eyelid, draw a small line up and out. Do both sides and try to get them the same as possible. Then, connect that line to the middle of the eyelid. Finally, draw along your eyelid to fill in the liner.

Glam witch icons: Beyoncé, Freddie Mercury, Amy Winehouse

Libra

Dates: September 23–October 22

Symbol: Scales

Element: Air

Planetary ruler: Venus

Modality: Cardinal

Tarot card: Justice

Color: Pink

Superpower: Why do Libras age so well? Surely it's not all Botox.

Beauty trick: Sunscreen absolutely must be a part of your skin care routine, regardless of your skin tone. Glam witch Libra babe Dita Von Teese doesn't leave home without it and wears gloves and hats to protect her skin from wrinkles and cancer. So buy sunscreen and put it on under your makeup in the morning.

Glam witch icons: Snoop Dogg, Bruce Springsteen, Kim Kardashian, Cardi B

Scorpio

Dates: October 23–November 21

Symbol: Scorpion

Element: Water

Planetary rulers: Mars and Pluto

Modality: Fixed

Tarot card: Death

Color: Black

Superpower: After each breakup, Scorpios go through full-blown transformations and somehow get hotter with each one.

Beauty trick: Your genitals aren't junk. They're what you use to make love and deserve their own beauty routine. So make sure to stay on top of sexual health and match your pubic hair to your style, whether it's a full-bush or laser hair removal. Get acquainted with yourself by using a hand mirror, and if you wax, do not forget your butthole.

Glam witch icons: Marie Antoinette, Adam Driver, Hedy Lamarr, Georgia O'Keeffe

Sagittarius

Dates: November 22–December 21

Symbol: Archer

Element: Fire

Planetary ruler: Jupiter

Modality: Mutable

Tarot card: Temperance

Color: Purple

Superpower: Ugh, I don't even want to give Sag the satisfaction of saying this, but you know how to get inside someone's head, don't you?

Beauty trick: Like an archer wielding a bow, Sagittarius knows the power of piercing. Just a quick pinch through the ears allows you to adorn your cartilage with diamonds—or the more affordable cubic zirconia.

Glam witch icons: Billie Eilish, Jimi Hendrix, Frank Sinatra, Britney Spears

Capricorn

Dates: December 22–January 19

Symbol: Sea goat

Element: Earth

Planetary ruler: Saturn

Modality: Cardinal

Tarot card: The Devil

Color: Brown

Superpower: Capricorns act like sociopaths, but be nice to them. There are lots of feelings under that hard exterior.

Beauty trick: Capricorn understands the power of dressing for the job you want, not the job you have. So fake it till you make it, bitch—costume is everything.

Glam witch icons: Elvis, Joan of Arc, David Bowie, Ricky Martin

Aquarius

Dates: January 20–February 18

Symbol: Water bearer

Element: Air

Planetary rulers: Saturn and Uranus

Modality: Fixed

Tarot card: The Star

Color: Blue

Superpower: An Aquarius knows how to dress for Coachella without culturally appropriating.

Beauty trick: Stand out by adding a pop of color to your makeup. For example, add a swipe of blue on top of a black winged liner, or swap out your usual nude lipstick for forest green.

Glam witch icons: Bob Marley, Yoko Ono, James Dean, Harry Styles

Pisces

Dates: February 19–March 20

Symbol: Fish

Element: Water

Planetary rulers: Jupiter and Neptune

Modality: Mutable

Tarot card: The Moon

Color: Aquamarine

Superpower: It's very easy to fall in love with a Pisces.

Beauty trick: Did you know that your bathtub is a giant cauldron? It's true. Just fill it up with water, bath salts, perhaps a nice fun bath bomb, and grab your weed or wine.

Glam witch icons: Rihanna, Elizabeth Taylor, Johnny Cash, Ruby Rose

Tarot Glamour

The Empress, along with such mythological counterparts as Aphrodite or Ishtar or Erzulie, represent something very grand. They signify the passionate approach to life.

—Rachel Pollack[26]

Want to know a secret? Understanding the tarot can make you a fabulous poker player. It's believed that what we call tarot cards originated sometime in the middle of the fifteenth century in Italy. The artist Bonifacio Bembo created a set for a game called Tarocchi for the bougie Visconti family of Milan. Back then, no one used it for divination. Instead, Tarocchi was a game for party tricks and gambling. But any poker player knows that it's not just about the cards that you're dealt. Instead, it's how you use glamour to outsmart everyone else at the table.

Through time and various adaptations by notable occultists, the cards, which were once used for fun fortune-telling, became divination tools. Don't get me wrong: any witch who says they don't use tarot to ask about what will happen with a crush is a liar, but divination is the least cool thing about tarot cards. Tarot cards are mirrors. They help you understand—and accept—what you already know. With that knowledge, you know how to best proceed.

The cards represent archetypes and show experiences or feelings that we've all had at various points in our lives. If you build a practice, you may notice that you begin to associate different cards with various points in time, people, or even places. People say that the Major Arcana represent life events, while the Minor Arcana show day-to-day experiences and emotions, the minor events that connect the big deals. Sure, but I find that it's more intuitive and fluid than that. Once you learn the cards, you know what they're saying. Often, I'll pull three cards, line them up, stare at them, and just let them speak to me about a specific subject. To help you on your couture tarot journey, here are some glamour witch hot takes on all the cards.

Major Arcana

The Fool: The Fool, the first card of the Major Arcana, represents beginnings and both childlike wonder and wisdom. The Fool wants you to try blue lipstick even when you're worried it looks ridiculous. (It doesn't.)

The Magician: The Magician is the card of manifestation and will-power. It tells us that we can get what we want using what we've got. The Magician wants you to dress like a rock star using your thrift store finds even when you're still an opening act.

The High Priestess: The High Priestess is the divine feminine we all contain, regardless of gender. She's an extraordinarily psychic and intuitive beauty with dark glamour. She wants you to go ahead and start kissing other girls.

The Empress: The Empress wears an iconic floral gown to show that she is a sex goddess. The card of primal sexuality, good news, and abundance, she wants you to know that it's OK if you gained a little bit of weight, and congratulations on being hot and thick.

The Emperor: The Emperor is a daddy and can be sweet like sugar, but he is very strict. The Emperor wants you to use condoms, wear sunscreen, and pay your taxes on time. Daddy knows best.

The Hierophant: The Hierophant represents churches, governments, and other ruling powers. Yet he is calm with spiritual wisdom. He says it's OK to get Botox. Seriously, everyone is doing it.

The Lovers: The Lovers are two annoyingly happy people in love who fuck each other's brains out daily. They want to let you know that it's normal and sweet to want to look pretty for your partner. Plus, if all of those assholes out there can find love, so can you.

The Chariot: The Chariot demonstrates that success is possible through willpower. It says that you can sculpt and tone your body if you just fucking go to the gym, but body positivity comes from within.

Strength: Strength shows a woman taming a lion, representing her inner emotional landscape. This card reminds us that having a good therapist is as important as having a good plastic surgeon.

The Hermit: The Hermit indicates that withdrawing temporarily from the outside world to restore inner calm is crucial. So for every party, date, or professional event you go to, make sure that you're making time to eat ice cream on the couch with your cat while binge-watching television.

Wheel of Fortune: The Wheel of Fortune reminds us that the only constant is change. So if you're down on your luck, fear not because you'll be on top of the world one day in the future. But conversely, if you just got a raise the same week you got engaged, remember that one day you'll be crying in the shower as the Notorious B.I.G. track "Mo Money Mo Problems" plays.

Justice: Justice sounds a bit scary, but it's just the card of fairness. If you've been treating your body like shit, you are going to have health problems, and if you're cheating on your partner, you're going to get caught. However, if you're living healthily, Justice brings good skin. It's the "you are what you eat" card.

The Hanged Man: No, the Hanged Man wasn't killed, nor did he kill himself. He's hanging upside down because he's the card of gaining wisdom through surrendering. The Hanged Man says that it's OK if your hair extensions come out during sex. Getting dirty is the whole point, and your partner will think it's hot!

Death: The Death card rarely represents a physical death but refers instead to a time of change and transformation. Breakups suck, but post-breakup glow-ups always make you hotter.

Temperance: Temperance is the card of patience and moderation. It also represents using rational thought to determine what moderation means to you. For example, Temperance wants you to know how many drinks make you charming and how many turn you into a bit of a psychopath.

The Devil: The Devil is a delightfully sinful card that understands that it's OK to be horny and vain. Sometimes, this card can point to the unhealthy habits holding you back. The Rider-Waite-Smith deck shows a couple—similar to the Lovers—standing beneath the devil with chains around their neck. However, upon examination, the chains are loose enough to take off—like good little submissives, they just don't want to. The Devil gives you permission to get another tattoo, but just not a matching one with the person you've been dating for three months.

The Tower: The Tower is a card of necessary destruction. It's getting fired from a job you hate or dumped by someone so wrong for you. It's a good card, but it hurts. The Tower says it's totally fine to get lip filler, but do your research and find a good doctor. Don't walk into some sketchy corner "med spa" that offers everything from hangover cures to vampire facials to Botox.

The Star: The Star is a very magical card of calm. It's finding joy and serenity after the chaos of the Tower. It's getting stoned while your face mask dries.

The Moon: The Moon indicates intuition, but also anxiety and projection. It's when you go through a massive breakup and then have a rebound and completely lose your shit when that ends because you never processed the first one. The Moon says that you can totally pull off that septum piercing and don't let your mother's voice get stuck in your head.

The Sun: The Sun card delivers a blast of youthful joy. It's petting a dog and understanding that beauty does exist in this world. Also, the Sun says that you'll look prettier if you take a vacation. It's gold eyeshadow brightening a winter day.

Judgement: Judgement calls for a spiritual leveling up. You don't have to start going to church, but it's time to stop dating losers. Judgement is when you finally accept that your natural deodorant doesn't work.

The World: The World completes the Major Arcana and signifies that you, too, are at a point of wholeness and accomplishment. The World reminds you that the contentment you experience in the afterglow of an orgasm exists all of the time.

Minor Arcana: wands

The Wands are pure firepower and, indeed, associated with the element of fire. If Wands were a song, it would likely be "Closer" by Nine Inch Nails. The energy of this suit is action. Wands are our primal selves in their truest form, and when manipulated through willpower, they help us manifest our dreams professionally and personally. But, just like your favorite fire sign friend, wands can be equal parts volatile and equal parts sex appeal. Problematic pop star and Sagittarius Taylor Swift was all Wands at the 2016 Met Gala, which she cochaired, wearing a metallic Louis Vuitton dress and boots, goth makeup, and a bleach-blonde bob. While still dating Calvin Harris, it's also the night she went viral for a dance-off with soon-to-be rebound Tom Hiddleston and allegedly met her current partner Joe Alwyn. All three men inspire hit songs and make the archer major bank on albums such as *Reputation* and *Lover*. So just like Tay and even Trent Reznor, you can harness Wands energy in your glamour routine by embracing your most chaotic, wild, and ambitious self.

King of Wands: The King of Wands is a CEO with big dick energy. He's a creative force, but he has minions to carry out his visions at this point in his life. He says that waxing your asshole is a great idea, but please, let a professional handle it.

Queen of Wands: The Queen of Wands is a confident boss bitch. She's very popular and has many friends. She says that getting your nipples pierced is a fantastic way to connect with your shadow side.

Knight of Wands: Passionate and impulsive, the Knight of Wands is chopping six inches off your hair after a breakup—and then going into the salon to have it fixed into a killer bob.

Page of Wands: The Page of Wands is that glorious period of inspiration and research before taking on a new opportunity. The Page of Wands is cool with you getting a boob job but wants you to take your time to study the various types of implants and review surgeons before going under the knife.

Ten of Wands: The Ten of Wands indicates that you are overworked and spread too thin. If you grant yourself permission to get a solid night's sleep or take a weekend off, your work will be better.

Nine of Wands: The Nine of Wands shows an injured man who is very weary but ready for war. He has only one more battle to endure before he can go home to peace and pussy. This card wants you to keep going; you're almost over the hump. It also suggests that life will be easier if you create firm boundaries. The Nine of Wands says not to be afraid to wash your hair when it needs it, even if a beauty blog told you only to do so once a week.

Eight of Wands: The Eight of Wands is swift movement and the momentum of an opportunity. You must strike while the iron is hot! If someone offers you a hair modeling gig, but you'll have to trade in your long brown hair for a trendy neon mullet, you should do it.

Seven of Wands: The Seven of Wands is a bit stressful. It's that anxious feeling when your life is going well, but it feels like everyone is after your job or trying to steal your man. In the Rider-Waite-Smith deck, the man is fighting a battle wearing two different shoes because he was unprepared for an onslaught. So how do you match your shoes and fight off the zombies? Confidence. The Seven of Wands says that you need a pair of heels that you can fight in. I recommend anything by Pleaser. They're shoes for strippers so that you can both dance and go to battle in them.

Six of Wands: The Six of Wands is a victorious card. Not only are you achieving goals, but you're receiving public recognition for your efforts. The Six of Wands wants you to wear a gown made of flowers while your cheating boyfriend burns in a bearskin straight out of *Midsommar*.

Five of Wands: The Five of Wands shows five people fighting for the hell of it or trying to collaborate and failing miserably due to their differences. It's a reminder that just because all of your friends are shaving their heads to embrace a queer identity doesn't mean that you have to. You're still gay with long hair.

Four of Wands: The Four of Wands indicates a joyful celebration, such as a wedding. It gives you permission to be a beautiful bridezilla, even if you are woke and queer.

Three of Wands: The Three of Wands is a card of opportunity. Life is going well, but you want more. So you gaze ahead at chances to create more abundance. The Three of Wands knows that investing in yourself and your appearance is an investment in your future.

Two of Wands: The Two of Wands maps out a success plan but shows no action has taken place yet. For example, going from black to platinum blonde in a single session is probably unrealistic, but if you're OK with a red phase and work with your colorist, your blonde ambitions can come true.

Ace of Wands: The Ace of Wands is a massive orgasm, a burst of passion and potential, that tells you that you are creative and intelligent enough to make your dreams come true. It says that if no skin care product speaks to you, you can create your own line.

Minor Arcana: cups

The Cups are the emotional tarot suit. They're the unconscious, psychic abilities we all contain. They are associated with the element of water. If the suit were a song, it would be "Waterfalls" by TLC: beautiful, intuitive, and filled with cautious emotion. If the element of water is emotion, then Cups are its container. Cups tend to refer to romance, sex, and relationships in a reading. They're also a nurturing suit, fueled by the divine feminine energy we all contain regardless of gender. Frank Ocean was flowing with Cups magick when he posted his legendary open letter on his Tumblr blog in 2012, discussing the forbidden queer love which inspired his atmospheric hit song "Thinkin Bout You." Not only did Ocean thank his unrequited first love, but also his friends and family for their support, stating, "I don't know what happens now, and that's alright. I don't have any secrets I need kept anymore. . . . I feel like a free man." As a result of his post, support flowed in from the likes of Beyoncé and Russell Simmons, and it became easier to be a queer man in hip-hop, helping open doors for the likes of Lil Nas X. Cups remind you that as above, so below. To look your best, you must feel your best and invest in supporting relationships as much as you do in skin care.

King of Cups: The King of Cups is calm and can control his emotions. This guy is proof that there are successful and emotionally available men out there. He reminds you not to cancel your friend just because she copied your manicure.

Queen of Cups: The Queen of Cups is an empathic and nurturing card. She wants you to feel your emotions and trust your intuition. So, for example, going gray is honorable and beautiful, but only if you're going to be a gray fox, not because you're scared people will think you're vain if you dye your hair.

Knight of Cups: The Knight of Cups is the quintessential knight in shining armor. He's a romantic and makes decisions from his heart rather than logic (relatable). Remember, if a man offers to buy you something, let him. It's feminist to let the patriarchy pay for your nose job.

Page of Cups: The Page of Cups is that moment when a brilliant idea just pops into your head seemingly out of nowhere. (Getting stoned helps.) When your drag queen or king name comes to you, you must seize the moment and work on makeup looks.

Ten of Cups: This is the happy relationship card. It's the sweet joy of a couple feeding one another wedding cake. It's becoming a couple who dress like one another and somehow pulling it off.

Nine of Cups: The Nine of Cups is a card of satisfaction. It's one of those rare moments where you're not full of dread, but actually like, "Hey, life is pretty good." So treat yourself to a massage.

Eight of Cups: The Eight of Cups shows a man walking away from a disappointing situation. Things didn't work out as he hoped, and he slinks off into the night discouraged. Yet leaving is the right thing to do, and the healing process will be more straightforward if he finally deals with his demons. Remember that a good therapist is as important as remembering to moisturize your neck.

Seven of Cups: The Seven of Cups is a card of both opportunity and illusion. Yes, you're dating again, but are you sure this person is good for you or are you just projecting? Remember that getting back together with your ex is usually a bad idea—and bad for your skin, too. So choose yourself and a good night cream (and ice cream!) instead of crawling into a former lover's dirty bed.

Six of Cups: The Six of Cups is a beautifully nostalgic card that indicates revisiting childhood memories. It also shows harmony and joy in your relationships, such as a childlike wonder. It's deciding to change your hair back to the color you had as a kid.

Five of Cups: Sometimes things just don't work out, but that doesn't mean your life is ruined. You're on the right path; you just need to stop fixating on the negative and look around at what else life has to offer. Maybe orange hair is a bit harsh for you, but there are so many shades of red that you can find a color that matches your passion and skin tone.

Four of Cups: Four of Cups means being so busy pouting you can't see the wealth, joy, and abundance that the world is offering. Sometimes you need a spanking to remember how gorgeous you are.

Three of Cups: The Three of Cups shows three friends dancing around having a drink. It's a card of celebration and is also the threesome card. So go to the spa or sex club with your best friends.

Two of Cups: The Two of Cups shows sexy new love. It's the NRE (new relationship energy) card—that giddy, orgasmic high that occurs at the start of a promising relationship. It permits you to stop work early to get ready for a date.

Ace of Cups: The Ace of Cups overflows with love and attention. It tends to signify the start of a new creative project or a blossoming romance. You're so filled with love that the only option is to share it with others. The Ace of Cups asks you to be honest and give your friend the tea when they ask about Botox, rather than raving on about your potent new eye cream like a liar.

Minor Arcana: swords

The suit of Swords represents the swift movement of pure logic. It's an intellectual suit that corresponds to the element of air. Swords use reason to slice through your enemy's bullshit like a knife through butter, but remember, Swords are double-sided. Too much power without empathy or a solid foundation can lead to inconsiderate actions and abuse of authority. If the suit of Swords were a song, it would be the industrial rock-pop "We Appreciate Power" by Grimes. According to a press release, the song was written "from the perspective of a Pro-A.I. Girl Group Propaganda machine who use song, dance, sex and fashion to spread goodwill towards Artificial Intelligence."[27] Yup, that sounds like something Elon Musk's baby mama would say—but the song still slaps.

When Aquarius legend Alicia Keys stopped wearing makeup on the red carpet in 2016, it was a revolutionary glamour move searing with Swords' softer side. However, she understands the importance of living by your own rules rather than those society imposes, later noting she hadn't made a permanent call one way or the other. "I'm not a slave to makeup. I'm not a slave to NOT wearing makeup either," the air sign told *Allure*.[28] In love, work, and glamour, Swords ask you to do what often can feel impossible: think with both your head and heart.

King of Swords: The King of Swords is wise and authoritative, even though he can come off as cold and calculating. It indicates that sometimes it's important to let someone else be the bad guy, such as a financial advisor, agent, or lawyer.

Queen of Swords: The Queen of Swords takes no bullshit. She can seem cold at times because she rules with logic instead of her emotions. Remember to take out your frustrations in a workout class rather than with tweezers to your eyebrows.

Knight of Swords: The Knight of Swords rages into battle, determined to conquer his dreams at all cost. However, he acts so quickly that this card can feel like rushing into a relationship based on good sex, only to realize that the loser still drunk dials his ex a month later. You can do better. A best friend and a vibrator can provide the emotional and physical support of a relationship while you take your time with dating.

Page of Swords: The enthusiastic Page of Swords is a sign of moving forward with brand-new ideas, but only if you intend to follow through. If you're going to take the time and money to get an old tattoo removed, at least attend all of your sessions so that it doesn't look like a faded mistake.

Ten of Swords: The Ten of Swords is a painful moment of defeat. The card shows a man on the ground, with ten blades in his back. The good news? There's nothing left to be stabbed with. Tarot readers frequently cite the phrase "it's always darkest before the dawn" with the Ten of Swords, so even though shit sucks right now, this is the last big ouch before things get better. It's time to pick yourself up and get some energy work done over those pain spots.

Nine of Swords: The Nine of Swords shows that horrible moment when you wake up in the dead of night and remember everything terrible you've ever done. You're anxious and worried, but your anxiety is causing more harm than what you're concerned about. Remember that negative thoughts can become a self-fulfilling prophecy. No, you're probably not losing your hair, but stress can cause hair loss.

Eight of Swords: The Eight of Swords shows a woman trapped in a shitty situation held captive due to her limiting beliefs. It's time to let those go. The gender revolution will only grow, so stop feeling like a fucking victim if you're a cis person and get with the program.

Seven of Swords: The Seven of Swords often shows up in memes these days, as it basically depicts a guy sneaking off from a party after stealing someone's weed. It's a card of deception, but are you the perpetrator or the victim? On its best day, the Seven of Swords is a before and after makeup transformation video. On its worst day, it's an "ethically nonmonogamous" guy who is just cheating on his girlfriend.

Six of Swords: The Six of Swords wants you to get over it. It's a time of transition, and sad as it is to leave a relationship in the past, it's time to drop your baggage and step into the present. The future holds so much. Get a pedicure and make sure they scrub off all of your dead skin and calluses. Then buy yourself a new pair of shoes as a treat.

Five of Swords: You know, we can't always win, and we're not always right. The Five of Cups indicates that you lost a battle and are bummed about it. Even worse—you probably deserved to lose this battle. Glamour witches know that it's essential to be open to when to own your mistakes and apologize.

Four of Swords: The Four of Swords shows the period after a breakup or leaving a job when you just really need to take a break from the world to rest and recuperate. Don't jump into a rebound relationship, but take yourself on vacation to reset and remind yourself that you're that bitch.

Three of Swords: This iconic card shows three swords piercing a heart. Oof, baby, someone hurt you. Indeed, the Three of Swords is the heartbreak card. However, like the stormy skies pictured behind the heart, this pain will not last forever—but you do need to get it out. Remember, it's glamorous to cry in fake eyelashes.

Two of Swords: The relatable Two of Swords depicts a woman sitting blindfolded, with two swords across her chest protecting her from harm. There is a decision to be made, but she's avoiding it. By burying her head in the sand, she prevents herself from getting all of the information pertaining to her and making a decision that will help her carry on in life. For instance, it sucks to sit down and make a budget, but your life will become much easier and more responsible after you do.

Ace of Swords: The Ace of Swords is an intellectual breakthrough. It's the card of new ideas and indicates that you're about to start a new project. It brings power, but as a giant blade appearing from the sky, it reminds you that it's up to you to use your energy wisely. Yes, you're hotter than you have ever been in your life and finally have the confidence to match. So are you going to go after your dream job or focus on making your enemies feel insecure?

Minor Arcana: pentacles

The Pentacles are all about, well, getting that coin. They're the grounded suit of possessions, security, and money. They correspond with the element of earth. Accordingly, in readings you can think of them as things we experience here during this lifetime. But, because our internal experiences shape our outside world, Pentacles also relate to creativity, confidence, and self-image.

If the suit of pentacles were a song, it would be "Bodak Yellow" by Cardi B.

In the video for "Bodak Yellow," Cardi B indeed wears the red-bottom Christian Louboutins she sings about. But, in her smash single, the Louboutins aren't new; the red bottoms are worn. If you ever go to a Christian Louboutin store, they tell you that Christian wanted the soles to be worn, so it's OK if the iconic red begins to rub off—still likely a tactic to encourage you to buy new ones in a year. But, when you usually see celebrities wearing them, that bottom is as clean and red as a fire truck freshly scrubbed down by hot firefighters.

Now, Cardi B buys red bottoms in bulk, but her first pair were given to her by an admirer in a strip club.[29] Cardi B wears worn Louboutins, even when we know she could get a fresh pair, because "Bodak Yellow" is all about her journey from rags to riches. That, witch, is Pentacles energy.

King of Pentacles: The King of Pentacles is a successful, wealthy daddy. He likely owns his own business. This card says that even if you voted for Bernie Sanders, it's OK to date a capitalist if he pays for things.

Queen of Pentacles: The Queen of Pentacles is the archetype of a working parent. She's successful, yet somehow also makes time to raise kids and make love to her partner. This card says it's OK to call the babysitter while you go get your roots touched up.

Knight of Pentacles: The Knight of Pentacles is a very reliable and hard worker, but he's also patient. So put your phone down and stop comparing yourself to people on social media. Instead, take that energy and put it into making your dreams come true.

Page of Pentacles: The Page of Pentacles stares at his coin, wondering how to turn it into more. The Page of Pentacles says that you can totally start a new business after thirty.

Ten of Pentacles: The Ten of Pentacles shows an accomplished person who is rich, surrounded by their family. Life is so good that they may not always understand how good they have it. You should visit your parents even if you did get an embarrassing matching hand tattoo with an ex that they'll ask about—especially if your parents paid for your college.

Nine of Pentacles: The Nine of Pentacles is a card of self-sufficiency and independent material success. So, if you can afford it, please, buy yourself some Christian Louboutins like Cardi B.

Eight of Pentacles: The Eight of Pentacles is a card of study and apprenticeships. If you continue to watch makeup tutorials and practice long enough, you can learn how to put on fake eyelashes.

Seven of Pentacles: The Seven of Pentacles shows a worker stepping back and admiring the fruits of his labor. It's a card that indicates hard work pays off, but it's also a reminder that it's OK to get that extra hour of sleep or take an occasional mental health day. You'll be more productive in the long run.

Six of Pentacles: The Six of Pentacles depicts a wealthy man handing out money to those with less than him, but let's call them sex workers for this book. Once again, the Six of Pentacles says it's chill to let a partner pay for your dinner and more. Oh, and save the guilt surrounding making money for billionaires.

Five of Pentacles: The Five of Pentacles shows a time of suffering, pain, and worry. Yes, things do suck, but you might be so trapped in your anguish that you fail to see that help is available. When things get terrible, it's fine to ask your mom for help paying for therapy or your partner for extra support.

Four of Pentacles: The Four of Pentacles represents a scarcity mindset. What's the point of having a little money if you can't have some fun? Buy yourself some new makeup brushes already, and get your mom flowers while you're at it.

Three of Pentacles: The Three of Pentacles shows the power of collaboration. Dressing up as Lady Gaga for Halloween is a fun idea, but you can make even bigger impact if your friends come too and you all go as a gaggle of pop stars.

Two of Pentacles: The Two of Pentacles is a card of time management. We see a man juggling multiple obligations and succeeding. So, if you're too busy to do your hair but want to look like Ariana Grande, invest in a clip-in ponytail extension to look glam in just a few minutes.

Ace of Pentacles: The Ace of Pentacles indicates a financial opportunity that may feel like it came out of nowhere. However, you must seize the day, take it, and follow through. That's why it's important to dress professionally, even in Zoom meetings—you never know what might happen!

3

BEAUTY SCHOOL

At the 2018 Met Gala, themed "Heavenly Bodies: Fashion and the Catholic Imagination," Solange Knowles carried Florida Water in her purse, which the artist paired with an Iris van Herpen latex dress—picked by her fans through a Twitter poll.[30] As many witches know, Florida Water cleanses negative energy. So the creative Cancer likely rightfully felt that she needed some extra protection around the fashion crowd.

The devil may wear Prada, but let's not malign Lucifer. The real evil in the fashion industry is sizeism, which *American Horror Story: Coven* star Gabourey Sidibe gave the middle finger to while looking like a Grecian goddess in a tranquil blue gown at the 2010 Academy Awards. And regarding skin and makeup, goddess Rihanna blessed us with Fenty Beauty in 2017, and her forty shades—now fifty—of foundation made the beauty industry finally address the issue of inclusivity.

But before the mainstream magazines caught on, witches were working in the hair industry for a long time, such as legendary Voodoo queen Marie Laveau. She worked as a hairdresser with white and Black clientele while slavery still existed. Lore suggests that she offered magickal services as well, using glamour to further both her businesses.

GLAMOUR WITCH

There's more overlap than an outsider might think regarding the glamour industry and glamour magick. For instance, did you know that pearls are not actually created from a tiny grain of sand but often from a parasitic worm infecting an oyster? And while diamonds are one of the hardest substances on Earth, due to their rigid tetrahedral crystal arrangement, their value is based on scarcity and manipulated by the corporations selling them.[31] Therefore, a witch must understand the realities of the glamour industries, such as jewelry, fashion, and makeup, so that you can use them to your advantage rather than get manipulated yourself.

It's delightfully fun and frivolous to understand how Botox works and fascinating that Cleopatra took milk baths for her skin, unaware at the time that milk does contain lactic acid, an alpha hydroxy acid that's used today to improve skin tone and texture. And while we celebrate vanity at Glamour Witch Beauty School, some tools—such as body modifications—have more political importance than removing wrinkles. For instance, gender affirmation surgeries allow trans and gender nonconforming folks to celebrate parts of themselves society has asked them to hide for years. So keep reading to learn the witchy, outrageous, and sometimes violent history all things glamour. And then, we'll infuse this knowledge into our spells and self-care rituals.

Clothing

Fashion is very important. It is life-enhancing, and, like everything that gives pleasure, it is worth doing well.

—Vivienne Westwood[32]

Clothing has the power to turn every day into Halloween. Morticia Addams certainly looks the part with her signature long black gown, matching dark hair, pale skin, and red lips. So does Nancy, the fan-favorite chaotic character from the 1996 film *The Craft*, in her nineties spiked choker, crucifix, plaid skirt, and black lipstick. Do you know why witches love black cats? It's so that their fur doesn't show up on our clothing.

While a little black dress is a must-have especially for witches, as Doreen Valiente, one of the founders of Modern Wicca, wrote in the 1978 book *Witchcraft for Tomorrow*, "the traditional attire of witches is generally believed to be nudity."[33] Think of the epic final scene in the 2015 film *The VVitch: A New-England Folktale*, where (spoiler alert) Anya Taylor-Joy ditches her clothing and religious family and goes flying into the air with a coven of witches, finally aware of her individuality and freedom.

But you don't need to be a nudist or a goth to dress like a witch. Dressing like a witch is all about wearing whatever makes you feel your most powerful. And, of course, there's color magick. Gabourey Sidibe, who starred in *American Horror Story: Coven*, made red carpet history at the 2010 Academy Awards in a stunning blue and silvery Marchesa gown, which draped like a garment made for a Greek goddess. As discussed in the color magick section, blue is associated with tranquility and protection, while silver represents the protective, intuitive, divine feminine—which we all contain regardless of our gender.

Sidibe wore the dress for her nomination for Best Actress in 2009's *Precious*. An Academy Award nomination is a really big deal, but the media and fashion industry focused much more attention on the star's body. Fox News ran a fatphobic and racist article with the headline "Gabourey Sidibe's Dress Mystery: When Plus Size Is Too Big for Hollywood,"[34] leading up to the event, and they weren't the only ones. Real glamour witches would never shame another for shining so brightly. The protective colors on her red carpet look came in handy, but the real reason Sidibe survived so much racist criticism is because she's powerful.

Sizing is mostly bullshit anyway. Size inflation is real, and those numbers tend to vary significantly from designer to designer. What's important is that a garment fits well. So never go with a size lower just for the sake of a number; always focus on what is flattering and comfortable. And if it bugs you, grab your magick scissors and snip out the tag! Problem solved. (Check out the Lord Byron Body Shame Banishing Spell in the Glamour for Money and Confidence chapter.) It's helpful to know your measurements, and, if you can, get apparel altered at a tailor to fit your unique body type.

One should dress as fabulously on the outside as you feel inside. A recent example includes the famous makeup artist Nikkie de Jager's—also known as NikkiTutorials—2021 Met Gala look, which paid tribute to LGBTQ+ rights icon Marsha P. Johnson. De Jager wore a floral headdress inspired by Johnson that also rocked major Empress card vibes. The light blue look also had a ribbon reading "Pay it no mind," which is the response Johnson would share with the press when asked about their gender.

But, of course, there are exceptions to the wear-whatever-you-want rule that must be addressed. Unfortunately, many of us are bound to workplace dress codes, the judgment of conservative relatives, and other reasons that encourage us to blend in as a form of protection work. In January of 2022, de Jager came out as trans—because she had to. "I have been blackmailed by people that wanted to leak my story to the press," she said in a YouTube video. "At first it was frightening. It was frightening to know that there are people out there that are so evil that they can't respect someone's true identity. It is vile and it is gross. And I know that you are watching this."[35]

In witchcraft, people ask a lot about the Rule of Three or the danger of a hex coming back to haunt you. No, you won't curse yourself if you cast a banishing spell on your abusive ex. But if you ever find yourself threatening to out someone, you may not even be a witch, but you definitely deserve all the toxic karma that will come your way. Hate crimes and harassment are not in a witch's toolbox, but fashion absolutely is.

Sometimes you need sweatpants, a face mask, and baseball hat to act as an invisibility cloak on the way to the pharmacy. Perhaps while growing up, you needed to wear more traditional clothing in order to survive and keep a roof over your head. And then there are those magical moments, such as a first date, wedding, or red carpet debut, when you want to look like the heartbreaker, queen, or rock star that you are.

And, as for the demon that whispers in your ear, "You can't pull that off," remember that the only trick to pulling something off is putting it on. Seriously, it's all confidence. When you need a boost, try listening to your power music while wearing the outfit in question. Let gods such as Josephine Baker or Freddie Mercury or even Frank Sinatra remind you of the power of doing it your way.

And, because going glam can cost a pretty penny, here are some more tips to get what you want for less.

+ Set up an eBay account. Search regularly for deals on your favorite products. You can find jewelry for pennies, designer shoes for sixteen bucks, and even Alexander McQueen ties for next to nothing.

+ Frequent secondhand shops. Thrift stores are the best place to get designer looks for less. What's more they're often vintage, baby, so you can feel as pretentious as you like. Wearing secondhand is also great for the environment, and if you live somewhere cold and love your fur, definitely opt for vintage.

+ Buy from online overstock or resale sites, such as The Real Real.

+ Host clothing swap parties. These are always such a ball! Once a month, gather your friends together and bring your old bras, T-shirts, and costumes. Swap for your friends' clothes that makes them bored but will be brand-new to you.

+ Use rotating closet services like Rent the Runway. Such subscriptions allow you to switch up your looks so that you don't become what the fashion blogs call a "repeat offender." And, if you love something, there's usually a pretty massive purchase discount.

+ Every now and then, we see an item that is simply Mr. Right. The dress, leather jacket, or corset simply worms itself into your brain, and you just have to have it—even if it's overbudget. Splurging on such pieces is usually worth it. Spending money on one black dress that you're obsessed with will save you money and make you happier in the long run than buying five other black dresses that cost less but you also like less.

Jewelry

Diamonds are intrinsically worthless, except for the
deep psychological need they fill.

—Nicky Oppenheimer, chairman of De Beers[36]

According to Lance Hosey of the *New York Times*, brain studies show that "the sight of an attractive product can trigger the part of the motor cerebellum that governs hand movement."[37] So instinctively, we reach out for pretty things; beauty literally moves us—all the more reason to embrace frivolity and frills no matter what day of the week it is. We are programmed to love shiny things—from Britney's navel ring to vintage engagement rings.

The oldest known jewelry to date was found in eastern Morocco, about 82,000 years old. The thirteen tiny shells were discovered in a cave. Around the same time, a sister set was found in a cave at the tip of South Africa. And pearls, considered the oldest gemstone, are produced inside the soft tissue of a living shelled mollusk.

Mythology connects pearls with the moon and goddesses. They are associated with Isis, the mother goddess in Egypt, and Xi Shi in China. Most people think that pearls are made from a tiny grain of sand—that's a cute fairy tale, but it's utter bullshit. In reality, pearls are more like kidney stones. A parasitic worm often infects an oyster, and when the oyster can't get rid of the thing, it coats it in pearly organic material until it turns into a smooth, shiny pearl. Talk about glamour magick! Because pearls are made of hexagonal crystal bricks with teeny gaps between them, pearls appear to glow from the inside out. This certainly caught the attention of Kokichi Mikimoto, a glamour witch whose name is now nearly synonymous with pearls.

Kokichi Mikimoto, born in 1858 in Japan, was utterly obsessed with pearls. His life's mission was to create a perfect pearl. Not only did he want an ideal pearl, but he wanted to make them accessible and affordable. First, Mikimoto discovered that he could create perfect spheres by wrapping an entire nucleus in living tissue taken from another oyster—the "all-lapped" technique. Then, he began farming them on a large scale. By the 1920s, he was also exporting pearls on a large scale. By his definition, as stated in a 1904 interview, "the cultured pearl . . . is obtained by compelling the pearl oyster to produce pearls. . . . [S]mall round pieces of nacre (mother-of-pearl) are inserted into the living oyster by a secret method." And then the oysters are put back in the sea and remain there for at least four years. They cover the inserted particle with their secretion during this time and thus form pearls. Yes, it causes the creature pain. Don't tell PETA or Kamala Harris, but pearls are not just pretty; they're pretty cruel.

The existing pearl industry was pissed. They'd been making loads of cash off their rare natural pearls, and here comes some guy who can not only sell more pearls at a lower cost, but they're perfect spheres. They went after Mikimoto, calling his pearls fake and attempting to shame anyone who dared spend money on his product. So what did he do? The only correct move there ever is when faced with controversy: he leaned in. He embraced the cultured pearl, marketed his pearls as cultured, and got in front of it so no one could say shit.

He was a bit dramatic. In 1932 he burned 720,000 "imperfect" pearls in front of a bunch of journalists, claiming they couldn't diminish the marketplace. If that sounds wasteful to you, here's a much cuter fact about pearl destruction: Octopuses eat pearls! Those smart, sneaky creatures are rolling around in the ocean with a belly full of coveted jewelry.

But while one may argue Mikimoto inflicted violence on mollusks, the quest for beautiful gemstones has affected entire groups of people due to colonization. For example, when the Spanish conquistadores went to the Americas searching for El Dorado, the legendary city of gold, the jewels they'd plunder weren't pearls or even gold, as legend states, but green. You see, the Inca believed that gold and silver were the sweat of the sun and the moon. They also thought emeralds were alive because they have a "vitreous luster" that makes the stones look wet. The luminescence made them appear divine, so emeralds weren't just worth a lot of money to the Inca; they were holy.

In 1543, the Spanish finally found a considerable lot of emeralds by cutting open the stomach of a hen, which was filled with tiny little gemstones. Chickens

eat small rocks to help them digest, and apparently, the ultraglamorous birds go for the emeralds just to shit them out. With the aid of disease on their side, the Spanish ultimately conquered the region and considered emeralds to be part of their winnings.

Why would one go through all the trouble of murdering a continent for some green stones? Well, as anyone with a nipple piercing knows, people are attracted to shiny objects, especially if they believe possessing them will help their status in society. We covet specific stones because they are scarce—or at least, as in the case of diamonds, we're told that they are. The island of Manhattan, which as of 2018 is worth $1.74 trillion, was purchased by the Dutch from the Lenape Indians in 1626 for glass beads and trinkets worth $24. But at the time, trade beads were commonly used by Venetians, and glass was a scarce commodity outside of Manhattan (known as New Amsterdam at the time). They were also beautiful and likely contained gorgeous swirling colors. The land was rather useless, so at the time, many suggested that the Lenape got the better deal.

And if you think that exchanging Manhattan for fucking glass is ridiculous, take a moment to consider your jewels. Did you know that Swarovski crystals are glass? Yes, the gems that Rihanna iconically wore as a dress are just glass, honey. And frankly, glass crystals and cubic zirconia often make a lot more sense than diamonds. Cubic zirconia (CZ) not only look like diamonds, but they are nearly as hard as diamonds—8.5 on the Mohs scale compared to a perfect 10. In addition, they're a fraction of the price, and even jewelry designers can rarely tell them apart. What tends to give CZ away is the cut and setting rather than the gem itself. Real diamonds are just a status symbol. In 1891, the diamond moguls De Beers intentionally slashed the production of diamonds by one-third in one year to cultivate the appearance of scarcity. After all, diamonds are carbon, an ultracompressed version of coal. But today, they can grow diamonds in a lab. So, if you want some but don't want mined diamonds, you can opt for science diamonds.

The Romans wore wedding bands and started the myth about the *vena amoris*, aka the "vein of love." This supports wearing a band on your ring fingers because it connects back to the heart. Technically this is correct, but then again, every vein leads back to your heart. So by this logic, a cock ring is just as romantic as a wedding ring. However, De Beers taught us that engagement rings should be diamonds, and not even that long ago. De Beers launched their "A diamond is forever" campaign in 1947. This Don Draper–approved advertising campaign is when the necessity of diamond engagement rings began popping off.

What is perfect about diamonds is their prism-like scattered light waves. The cubic lattice is perfectly symmetrical in every direction and, as a result, scatters light waves that look like rainbow sparkles. The rest? It's mostly mythology. Ironically, the same conservative diamond slinger will make fun of someone for wearing a rose quartz necklace to attract love while trying to pawn a diamond ring for $30,000 because it's considered a sacred monogamy stone. Crystals, gemstones, talismans—whatever name you call them—do have a role in glamour magick. Working with rose quartz does provide many witches with a dose of sweet love, and there can be something sacred about wearing a ring to demonstrate your devotion to another. But you can get your sparkle on without giving your entire savings over to the diamond district. Practice smart glamour with the following tips:

+ Buy diamonds if you like, but remember there is no shame in opting for CZ.

+ If you love piercings, one place you should not cut corners with is the metal used. Sure, it can be adorned with CZ, but only let surgical stainless steel, 14k or 18k gold, titanium, or niobium in your healing holes. Avoid copper or gold cut with too much copper, as it will turn your ears green.

+ If a lover gives you jewelry and you like it, you must wear it. It's positive reinforcement that will encourage them to buy you more jewelry.

+ Mixed metals are in! Mix it up, layer it up, have fun with your jewels, and don't follow any silly old rules.

+ Jewelry is not just for women. All genders and orientations should adorn themselves!

+ Keep your jewelry organized. It's so easy to lose. Buy a jewelry organizer, and to be extra careful, use some of those tiny baggies that they sell cocaine in to store earrings.

+ Always close the sink before putting on earrings in front of the bathroom mirror.

+ If you're dating someone you'd like to marry, make sure to inform them of your ring size. It's OK to be sneaky about it! All is fair in love and war. I suggest buying yourself a ring—it can just be costume jewelry—and ensuring that your beau is present when you measure your band size.

Skin

*We are all sculptures and painters, and our material is our
own flesh and blood and bones.*

—Henry David Thoreau[38]

As we learned in grade school, the skin is the largest organ in the body. When stretched out, it can encompass twenty feet. It's a canvas for makeup and tattoos. It also ages, and even with regular Botox, your skin will change with time and there's nothing anyone can ultimately do about that. But of course, inherently vain as we are, that doesn't mean we haven't tried.

In 3000 BCE, the beauty-conscious Egyptians created anti-wrinkle cream from olive oil, ostrich eggs, dough, and essential oils. One of their star ingredients was frankincense, which supposedly has anti-inflammatory properties. Its use is so tied to spiritual practices that the New Testament even mentions frankincense as one of the three gifts along with gold and myrrh presented to Christ as gifts. Modern-day witches often use frankincense as a purifier, much like sage or palo santo.

Egyptian glamour witch Cleopatra was particularly fond of her milk baths, which she infused with honey and herbs, so she was obviously aware of the power of bath magick. Cleopatra clearly had a strong intuition. While they didn't know it at the time, milk contains lactic acid, an alpha hydroxy acid that's used today to improve skin tone and texture. In 1995, after decades—or millennia if we appropriately credit Cleopatra—AHAs were recognized for their ability to decrease fine lines and wrinkles. They're most often used in facial and chemical peels.

There is one demon within the skin care industry that must be called out, and that's skin-lightening creams. For most of U.S. history, skin-whitening products were sold to both white and Black women. Not only did this uphold white supremacy, but a pale white face indicated that you were rich enough to sit on your ass inside all day. Upsettingly, early ads depict a painting of a frowning Black woman, who in the next photo transforms into a smiling light-skinned woman through the power of Lucky Brown skin lightener. Today, skin-whitening creams are enduringly popular in Asian markets. In China, skin whitening accounts for 30 percent of the total skin care market.[39] While it's alarming to think about skin-whitening products, we can remember that, historically, many people of color used them as a protection spell. Regardless of how damaging such products are to the skin, or if they even work, they advertised fitting in within a white supremacist culture. The folks who used them didn't want to be white ladies: they just didn't want to get killed.

And if whitening creams weren't enough, skin care products and makeup for Black women in the United States were basically nonexistent until recently. When Rihanna launched Fenty Beauty in 2017 in partnership with LVMH, her forty shades—now fifty—of foundation made the beauty industry finally address the issue of inclusivity.[40] The industry standard quickly changed, with competitors such as Kylie Cosmetics debuting a new line of concealers in thirty shades shortly thereafter.[41]

But, of course, glamour witches were always brewing something up. Around the 1920s, women such as Madam C. J. Walker and Annie Turnbo Malone launched companies with products for darker-skinned women and opened doors for fellow Black entrepreneurs to find success in skin care. In fact,

historians say that the Black beauty industry matured before the white trade did.[42] Somewhat ironically, around the same time, known Nazi Coco Chanel popularized the suntan and made darker skin desirable for white folks after getting accidentally burned on vacation in the French Riviera. If you have pale skin, don't be like Coco: protect that goth complexion.

Sunscreen was invented in 1935. Think of it as a protection spell: wear it daily, even during the winter. While people of color have been largely left out of sunscreen studies,[43] the medical consensus is that all races should wear the stuff. According to the American Academy of Dermatology, you should opt for at least an SPF 30—which blocks 97 percent of the sun's UVB rays[44]— and apply it to your face, décolletage, and hands, which are all literally thin-skinned and show the effects of sun damage. And, if you're rocking that bikini body on the beach—and note, too, that all bodies are bikini bodies!—rub it everywhere. Sun exposure also causes cancer. Plus it ruins tattoos!

Beyond racist skin-whitening creams, there are still plenty of ways to harm your skin. Early wrinkles are something even those of us ready to naturally age into a crone stage like to avoid.

The following can cause damage to the skin:[45]

Smoking

Yes, Zelda Spellman makes cigarettes look glamorous as hell, but try to avoid them. Even nicotine alone can hurt your skin by causing blood vessels there to contract, so sadly, vaping won't save you. In fact, cocaine, caffeine, or anything that restricts the blood vessels can be damaging. (Of course, if you're prescribed amphetamines, don't put your mental health at risk by going off your meds just to keep from aging your skin.)

Sun Exposure

Listen up, vampires. Buy sunscreen, stat. Not only does sun exposure lead to early wrinkles, but it can cause skin cancer. Sun molecules, which you've probably heard cause free radicals, can damage the DNA of your cells, which in addition to skin concerns, can cause heart disease. Sunscreen is a must. Neutrogena's Ultra Sheer Dry-Touch is a great drugstore find.

Drinking Too Much

Too much alcohol makes you act like a child, but it does the reverse to your skin. It can also cause free radicals to form and depletes the body of crucial nutrients. Do you know that parched, painful, what-have-I-done feeling during a nasty hangover? Your skin feels the same way. Head to the spell section to learn how to brew a witchy tea to drink as an alternative.

Overall Nutrition

If you needed an excuse to stop yo-yo dieting, know that taut, underweight skin looks like crap. All that stretching back and forth of losing weight and gaining weight is bad for you, so don't do it! Witches come in all sorts of body types, and all witch bodies are good witch bodies.

Sleep

I have fantastic news for you. Lack of sleep can cause wrinkles! That means that getting a long night of beauty sleep is a must; you're not lazy at all. Getting plenty of sleep is responsible. We'll talk more about sleep as self-care, including how to do magick in your dreams, in the spell section of this book.

Genetics

Yes, some people just age better than others. And sorry, fellow white chicks, but we tend to develop wrinkles sooner than other races. While you can't change your genes, you can work with ancestors to embrace your unique beauty.

Stress

Don't date losers. It's terrible for your skin. Opt for a love spell and relaxing breathing techniques over a partner who gives you more frown lines than orgasms.

In addition to knowing what to avoid, everyone should have a solid morning and night skin routine. It's easy to spend too much money on skin care only to be unsure of what goes where.

The following are general steps for a day and night beauty routine. Reference these as you would a spell until you learn them by heart:

Day

1. Cleanser

2. Toner

3. Antioxidant serum

4. Eye cream

5. Spot treatment

6. Lip cream (with SPF)

7. Moisturizer

8. Sunscreen

9. Makeup

Night

1. Makeup remover (I start with a makeup removing wipe, and then use a Q-tip and bottled remover to get what's left behind on my eyes.)

2. Cleanser

3. Toner

4. Serum and treatments

5. Retinol

6. Eye cream

7. Lip cream (without SPF)

8. Night cream

9. Face oil

Hair

You can't touch my hair.

—Phoebe Robinson[46]

Let's forget about Salvador Dalí for a moment—although his paintings are dope and that mustache is iconic. The original Dali is a Georgian goddess who serves as the patron of hoofed wild mountain animals. She was also a jealous bitch who herself tended to be successful on the prowl. She was described as a beautiful nude woman with golden hair—sometimes even literal gold—and glowing skin. If she wore anything on her body, it was gold jewelry to match her mane. She was so beautiful—especially that hair!—that it drove the hater humans mad, although that didn't thwart Dali's fondness for taking on human lovers, who, yes, ended up dead from time to time. Some mortals' deaths sound deserved, though. Many tales depict hunters trying to cut off Dali's hair as part of a rape attempt in the forest. So naturally, those idiots had to go.

Hair has power, which humans readily use for evil—and sadly not just against Dali's attempted rapists. It's why some witches keep careful track of their hair clippings. That way, your enemy can't use your hair in a hex against you. Spells using hair include braiding spells directly into your braids—often as a form of protection—adding clippings of a lover's or enemy's hair to a spell such as a potion or a candle to ensure they do your bidding. In the Victorian era, women had little pots on their vanity to stash their own loose hair, which they'd use to create hairpieces called rats. If this disgusts you—or you don't shed enough hair to do so—you can inexpensively purchase hairpieces to mold your hair into bumper bangs, chic buns, victory rolls, and more. Sometimes, all glamour witches must opt for store-bought.

What happened under colonialism is far more sinister than saving a former lover's pubes for a protection spell. For instance, the Europeans knew how precious hair is when they began the Atlantic slave trade in the early sixteenth century. It's why they shaved their captives' heads to sever them from their ancestors, homeland, and personal expression. We see this same evil act in the shaven heads of those six million Jews who died in concentration camps and other horrible ways during WWII. Before we write off these actions as a thing of the past, it's important to understand that this still happens today. The Chinese shave prisoners' heads in "political reeducation camps"—also known as the Xinjiang internment camps—set up by the Chinese Communist Party. According to Human Rights Watch, these camps predominantly target Muslims and have been criticized for alleged human rights abuses, including rape, torture, and even genocide.[47]

In the United States, Black women are still underrepresented in the beauty market and risk losing work if they wear their natural hair. Black women are 1.5 times more likely to be sent home from work because of their hair. In 2019, thirty-two-year-old Brittany Noble, a former news anchor at a local station in

Jackson, Mississippi, was fired after filing formal discrimination complaints regarding her hair. "After having my son, I asked my news director if I could stop straightening my hair," she wrote. "A month after giving me the green light I was pulled back into his office. I was told, 'My natural hair is unprofessional and the equivalent to him throwing on a baseball cap to go to the grocery store.' He said, 'Mississippi viewers needed to see a beauty queen.'"[48] Oh, honey. Deciding what a crown looks like and who wears it is not up to you. Mut, a mother goddess in ancient Egypt, wore a double crown of the kings. Yes, the double crown of *kings*—sorry, Mississippi news director—which represented her power over the entire land. But folks today aren't even asking to wear two crowns, just their natural hair. Thank you very much.

Progress is happening, although much more is needed. For example, the CROWN Act (Create a Respectful and Open World for Natural Hair) was written in 2019 by Dove and the CROWN Coalition in partnership with former state senator Holly J. Mitchell of California. This legislation ensures protection against discrimination based on race-based hairstyles by extending statutory protection to hair texture and styles such as braids, locs, twists, and knots in the workplace and public schools. It passed unanimously in both chambers of the California Legislature in 2019. Similar bills are currently in the works in other states.[49]

While oppressed people must fight to wear their natural hair, others voluntarily go through torture to modify theirs. As with everything, the pain of beauty is only glamorous if it is consensual. For instance, going blonde has always been a bitch. In the fifteenth century, Venetians and Romans covered their heads in a mixture containing quicklime, sulfur, honey, white grapes, walnut flowers, elderberries, lupine, and myrrh. It sounds like a recipe to summon a demon. Then, just like we do today at salons with much more efficient lamps, they stuck their heads in the sun for several days. The result was scarring, being smelly, burned scalps, and reddish-blonde tresses with a side of sunstroke.

As depicted in the painting *Hylas and the Nymphs* by John William Waterhouse, red hair can be seen as a sign of evil. The nymphs have loose red hair, which suggests their dangerously seductive nature. Additionally, while hair

dye came in fashion (usually blonde or black), red hair carried connotations of witchcraft and prostitution during the Crusades. Oh, hello, Nicole Kidman's character from *Practical Magic*. Auburn became popular during the Elizabethan era, although never as popular as a blonde. Rhubarb steeped with wine or lye lightened hair but damaged it. A safer alternative of the time was turmeric and alum, which produced a darker blonde. This extreme take on beauty as pain is an early example of color magick. As we find with the good witch Glinda, blonde has always represented purity and rarity—with an occasional dose of white supremacy. While blonde is still desirable today, the one light hair color people have avoided for millennia is gray.

Around 3400 BCE, the ancient Egyptians started applying henna to their roots to cover grays. Gray hair is as certain as death and taxes, so one has two options. Whether you're inspired by witches such as the Russian wild woman Baba Yaga or silver fashion fox Tim Gunn, you can lean into your inner crone.

Or are you more of a Dolly Parton give-no-shits-about-natural kind of witch? Then dye it and save the guilt for the Chinese government and colonizers. The first recipes for dyeing hair black occurred in 100 CE, thanks to Roman Empire doctor Claudius Galen, who wrote about a mixture of lead oxide, slaked lime, and boiled walnuts and leeks. Back then, men didn't deal with the same gendered stigma regarding hair that they do today. Looking fabulous wasn't just about being pretty, either—it made you a warrior.

The Vikings, the infamous seafaring Scandinavians of the eighth to eleventh centuries known for their masculinity, carried hair kits, containing custom combs for hair and beards, as well as tweezers to keep their eyebrows on fleek. They tied their long luscious hair back during battle to make sure it didn't get bloody. It was even against the law to cut someone's hair short without his consent. Their attention to glamour terrified the pasty English. The monk John of Wallingford wrote, "In the habit of combing their hair every day, to bathe every Saturday, to change their clothes frequently and to draw attention to themselves by means of many such frivolous whims ... they sieged the married women's virtue and persuaded the daughters of even noble men to become their mistresses."[50] It sounds less like these women were helpless victims of brutal Vikings, and more like they finally met some men who could lay the pipe.

The most famous wigmaker in France, Georges Binet, kept Norman women of Viking descent on retainer to grow hair. Before we continue with the story, it's worth noting that modern hair traders comb places such as Chinese and Indian villages searching for women who want or have to sell their hair because of extremely limited work options. A popular destination for hair-buyers—real hair does in fact make for better quality extensions than synthetic hair—are Hindu temples in South India, where pilgrims sacrifice their hair in a practice called tonsuring. And yes, if you're wondering, the ethics are questionable. Fresh hair cut directly from a woman's head gets the highest price and is commonly referred to as "black gold" by traders. According to 2018 data, hairdressers in Myanmar's largest city of Yangon were offering between $11 and $150 for a head of hair—anywhere from four to fifty-five times the country's minimum wage of $2.70. So, while these people's hair is certainly worth more, their decision is more than understandable and a statement on world wealth disparity, not to ruin your new Ariana Grande-style clip-in pony, or anything.[51]

But before Khloé Kardashian was showing off her closet dedicated purely to hair extensions on Instagram, we had Binet, the guy who gave King Louis

XIV (1638–1715) a wig made from ten heads of Viking hair. Louis XIV popularized wigs in Europe. You see, his hair was falling out, perhaps due to syphilis. (Fun fact: The side effects of syphilis not only contributed to the popularization of wigs, but techniques in rhinoplasty as well, as you'll learn about in the Body Modifications section. Always opt for Western medicine when dealing with a case of the syph.) Wigs became his signature look, and he had an entire room dedicated to them—a royal wig glamour altar, just like Khloe. Before Louis discovered wigs and hooked up with Binet, wigs tended to be crappy little things reserved only for the old and sickly. But after Louis XIV rocked his, wigs were flying off the shelves. Before too long, the trend spread to England and then, within a decade, all of Europe. The trend also helped establish France's reputation as a fashion epicenter, although France is far from the only place to recognize the power of the wig.

Ancient Egyptians not only wore elaborate wigs on their heads but on their faces too. Beard wigs were a common sight on rulers such as Ramses the Great. But the people who really know how to rock a wig are the Huli tribe or Wigmen of Papua New Guinea. Their whole culture is built on glamour. They wear opulent wigs made from their own hair with no hair-mining of poverty, so the bigger the wig, the stronger the man. They also used hair ornaments, such as the bird-of-paradise flower, and go all out on makeup. Birds-of-paradise are as glam as it gets for floral hair adornments, and these guys aren't even culturally appropriating. If you've never seen the flower up close, it's a spiked, vivid orange, complete with blue decorations. It's a flower that's more punk than a mohawk sighting in Manchester. But that's not even the best part. Bachelor Wigmen perform spells to ensure that their hair grows lusciously and to protect their wigs. Often respected spiritual elders would bless younger men to help their hair grow. As a glamour witch knows, a proper mentor can be hard to find!

Some hairstyles are universal in their glamour. While it's true that the bird-of-paradise plant gives it a run for its money, the mohawk is the ultimate warning sign. Before the punks wore it, Native American tribes were known for the cut. However, it appears that societies recognized the fierce spirit of the mohawk all over the world. A preserved body from Ireland named Clonycavan

Man wore a mohawk, and the Roman Empire rocked helmets adorned with mohawks made from feathers or horsehair. Today, the mohawk—along with the faux hawk and side shave—are classic queer haircuts. In 2020, shortly after calling off their engagement, queer pop star and alien hunter Demi Lovato debuted a blonde faux hawk. A queer breakup mohawk? Yes, please.

But before the days of proudly displaying your new queer 'do on Instagram, once upon a time it was only safe to come out to other gays. And hair held a significance position in that regard. Before World War II, socialite gays came out at drag balls modeled after the debutante balls—those events where a father throws a party signaling it's time to marry off his daughter. But, of course, few fathers were going to throw their gay son a ball at the time, so they organized their own! They didn't use the phrase "coming out," but instead "dropped hairpins" to signal that they were gay. Wearing one's hair up referred to fitting into heteronormative society, and letting one's hair down referred to letting one's queer self rock. "The coming out of new debutantes into homosexual society was an outstanding feature of Baltimore's eighth annual frolic of the pansies," read a spring 1931 *Baltimore Afro-American* article.[52] Drag balls continue in the present, influenced mainly by the Black gay men and trans folks of New York City during the AIDS crisis during the 1980s and '90s. And, of course, these very real scenes are the inspiration for the hit FX drama *POSE*.

As there is always contrast in glamour, while we often try to make the hair on our head look more prominent, there are many ways one can remove body hair as well. But, of course, if you feel more powerful with body hair, keep it. For those who get off on self-imposed pain, let's review hair removal options.

Shaving

Glam: Shaving is fast, cheap, and easy.

Scam: Red bumps are always cause for concern on the genital region, and "It's just an ingrown hair" will always sound suspicious! Not to mention, day two brings in the waltz of the prickly pussy.

Waxing

Glam: Waxing lasts longer than shaving, and the more you do it, the less the hair grows back in.

Scam: It hurts like a bitch.

Electrolysis and Lasers

Glam: Both electrolysis and lasers detach the hair from the follicle and zap away the follicle itself. Electrolysis uses shortwave radio frequencies in hair follicles to stop new hair from growing, while laser therapy uses mild radiation via high-heat lasers. While some hair may grow back thinner—mine did—after six treatments the hair should be permanently gone.

Scam: You better be sure that you want bare genitals before you go for something more permanent. It's much more expensive than shaving, but if you added up all the money spent on hair removal in your life, you might save.

Depilatories

Glam: This is the Nair hair-removal products that you associate with moms of times past. It's a chemical that dissolves the bonds in the keratin of the hair and makes a great option for those superprone to ingrown hairs caused by shaving.

Scam: They can bother sensitive skin and sometimes stink of rotten eggs. It feels old-fashioned and not in a fun psychotic housewife way.

Threading

Glam: Threading's been done for thousands of years. It's easy, safe, and especially effective for one area of the face, such as the eyebrows or upper lip area.

Scam: It's not really something one does around the butthole.

Sugaring

Glam: This is not a reference to sugar babies. Sugaring uses sugar (or honey), lemon juice, and water that form a natural paste. It hurts less than waxing.

Scam: Sugaring doesn't last as long as waxing, and it's trickier to get each hair.

Makeup

You are not born glamorous. Glamour is created.
—Max Factor[53]

What's the witchiest makeup brush? Now, a contour brush is crucial, but hake brushes—traditional Japanese paintbrushes made with devilish goat hair—take the cake due to their horned origins. They're also an integral part of the application process that transforms *Wicked* Broadway actors into Elphaba's signature green skin. Believe it or not, Broadway makeup artist Craig Jessup can complete the transformation in eighteen minutes. In Universal's film adaptation of the hit musical *Wicked*, actor Cynthia Erivo will play Elphaba. Fans applauded the casting of a woman of color as Elphaba, a character that often goes to white actors despite this being misaligned for her skin tone. Naturally, Cancer queen, Ariana Grande will play good witch Glinda.[54]

Grande knows a thing or two about makeup, having launched her own brand, r.e.m. beauty, which came out in November of 2021. Grande may be a Cancer, but her beauty brand is all Scorpio, baby. Star products include the "on your collar" plumping lip gloss in iridescent lavender, which will indeed leave heavenly shimmer kisses on your lover's collar—or white panties or packing dildo.[55] After all, all genders and orientations should enjoy the power of a glitter lip. The Neanderthals didn't have makeup hang-ups, and they invented glitter! All genders would use foundation, and highlighter, which they made from ground up pyrite, their genius glitter ingredient.[56] Pyrite is also known as fool's gold. Like the sunshine it resembles, pyrite is associated with abundance and joy. However, whether you're using glitter for makeup or to dress a spell candle, store-bought is fine. Remember that most glitter is made with microplastics—which are a problem for the environment—so opt for a sustainable brand, such as Electrik Glitter,[57] sourced from eucalyptus trees.

Homo sapiens makeup use dates back 7,000 years and is found in every society known to Earth, so it's safe to say your makeup obsession is totally normal. The Egyptians understood a union between the physical and the spiritual and left medical texts containing over 700 recipes for grooming and wellness. But what might be even more incredible is that all genders embraced the holiness of makeup. Sure, you've heard of Cleopatra, but what about Ramses the Great? This Egyptian ruler was primped and polished with only the best skin care and makeup of his time. Ramses the Great even had one servant whose title was "Chief of the Scented Oils and Pastes for Rubbing His Majesty's Body." Ramses, like his culture, believed that the better you looked, the more the gods loved you.

Among the Egyptians' go-to looks were black kohl eyeliner and red ocher for rouge and lips. Anyone who rocks a cat eye—hello, Nina Simone!—can thank the god Horus with his iconic Eye of Horus, an elaborate kohl outlined eye. Today, the Eye of Horus is used mainly as a protection symbol, although its makeup inspiration lives on. The Egyptians' staples prove that red lips and black eyeliner have always been sexy far before Taylor Swift caught on. And if the Egyptians can understand that spirituality and vanity are intertwined,

perhaps it's time that we admit that witchcraft and science can not only coexist but help make sense of one another. For example, scientists know that seeing red increases heart rate, blood pressure, and hunger. Perhaps this is why cultures worldwide utilize the power of the red lip.

In Japan, the geishas—high-class entertainers expertly trained in multiple arts—practiced makeup looks that are still iconic today. These include an arching red lip, pale white face, and red accented eyes. While their unique eyeshadow looks utilize *Euphoria*-level creativity, one makeup trick modern artistes will likely not be co-opting is the tradition of painting the teeth black using recipes containing bird droppings. While geishas weren't sex workers, after the Edo period (1603–1867) only geishas, actual sex workers, and aristocratic men blackened their teeth. It was simply too much work—and well, smelly—for your everyday lady. Witches use honey on our lips to sweeten our words. And even though teeth-blackening was ornamental—although there may have been protective dental reasons as well—maybe a little bird droppings along the teeth did help those geishas spray some verbal shit if anyone in their company got the wrong idea.

Asian cultures such as those of Korea, Japan, and India viewed bathing as godly, and as a result, they have historically been ahead in the beauty game. Sixth-century Korean warriors, the *hwarang*, wore smoky eyes and red eye-shadow to win favor from the gods in battle while protecting their kingdom, just like the Vikings paid attention to their hair. Aesthetics were interwoven with their perceived abilities as soldiers. The *hwarang* also rocked pierced ears and high-end clothing. As one text describes, "They selected the handsome boys of nobility and adored them, powdering their faces and calling them Hwarang. The people of the country all respected and supported them."[58] Far before BTS, the Koreans were already building their reputation for creating beautiful men with great skin. It's a far cry from the sallow strictness of the Puritans. Throughout history, Christians viewed bathing as too close to vanity. There's a reason why the only hot people in the 2015 film *The VVitch* set in 1630s New England are Anya Taylor-Joy, of course, and the witch of the woods who uses smashed babies as a form of glamour magick–infused body cream.

But Hollywood adaptations aside, the birth of Christianity marked a shift in attention from the body to the soul. While one would think they are intertwined, this division gave permission to label adornment as vanity and therefore sinful. The Bible even mentions makeup. Cosmetics are in the Old Testament in 2 Kings 9:30–31, which reads, "Then Jehu went to Jezreel. When Jezebel heard about it, she put on eye makeup, arranged her hair, and looked out of a window. As Jehu entered the gate, she asked, 'Have you come in peace, you Zimri, you murderer of your master?'"

He did not come in peace. They threw Jezebel out the window to die and let horses trample her to finish the job. Her name eventually became synonymous with being a big whore, in part because of her affinity for makeup. Indeed, historically, the group who continued wearing makeup despite the hate was sex workers. Regardless of what you do for money, wearing all the makeup you want is a great way to filter out unsuitable lovers. Only alphas can handle a witch in full beat.

While Christian societies can still have negative associations with makeup, you always had a free pass if you were rich. Queen Elizabeth I was the queen of England and Ireland from November 1558 until she died in 1603 and the last of the five monarchs of the House of Tudor. And Lizzy loved her makeup. During her reign, cosmetics became more acceptable. Even nuns curled and powdered their hair. The Tudors brought abundance, and as a result, cosmetics such as hair dye, rouge, and a gothic white face were in—but at a price. The royalty's beloved face paint was often made with ceruse, a white lead known as Spirits of Saturn. Legend states that Elizabeth I's coffin even exploded due to the poisonous fumes rising from her decaying corpse.

Now, one group of people who gave the geishas a run for their money when it comes to the art of a paste-white face was the *macaroni*. The term pejoratively referred to a man who "exceeded the ordinary bounds of fashion" in terms of clothes, food, and vices. These fashionable fellows lived in mid-eighteenth-century England and dressed and even spoke in an outlandishly affected manner. Think faces caked in white makeup, lavish blush, and two-foot-tall wigs. People hated the poor macaroni, and not just because of their overstated wealth. Many of these well-dressed darlings were gay in a time when you really couldn't be gay. They also triggered some early transphobia. The March 1772 edition of *Town and Country Magazine* wrote: "There is indeed a kind of animal, neither male nor female, a thing of the neuter gender lately started up among us." They are even made fun of in the song "Yankee Doodle," in the line "He stuck a feather in his hat and called it macaroni." Thanks for teaching us at an early age that men can be fabulous, America. Macaroni culture later influenced "dandies," who bent a bit more to gender expectations at the time while still looking glam.

The Victorians even criminalized male beauty during the late 1800s with the Criminal Law Amendment Act of 1885, a set of laws in the UK that went after gays and sex workers. But, of course, just like today's FOSTA-SESTA legislation on sex trafficking, they mostly were passed under the guise of protecting women and minors. In 1924 London, a man named Thomas B. served three months in prison for having a "lady's powder puff, powder, and a small mirror." Another fellow, poor William K., served nine months of hard labor kicked off with a whipping for possessing "face powder, scented handkerchiefs, and two photographs of himself in woman's [sic] costume."[59]

The nineteenth century, however, was pivotal for makeup, mainly due to one major technological breakthrough: the mirror. People finally could see clearly what they looked like au naturel. In 1835, the German chemist Justus von Liebig developed a process for applying a thin layer of metallic silver to one side of a pane of clear glass. In a historical moment for vanity, mirrors became widely available. Everyone finally noticed their undereye circles and demanded access to glamour tools. This moment was as significant for the ego as the rise of the selfie. Before that, the only people who regularly saw themselves on camera were the stars.

The iconic makeup brand Max Factor was created by Maksymilian Faktorowicza, who escaped anti-Semitic Russia thanks to his talents. He was so good that he worked as the Russian royal family's prized hair and makeup artist. But despite his gifts, he was also a Jewish immigrant with a family he kept secret, as none of them were safe in the country. Max escaped his employers by using his makeup skills to create a sickly look with yellow tones. He got some

time off work, and boarded the SS *Moltka* with his family to start a new life in the United States. Maksymilian Faktorowicza was shortened to Max Factor at Ellis Island, and he settled in St. Louis in 1904 selling homemade face creams at fairs. After his wife died and his business partner stole his savings, Max was ready for another fresh start and headed to Los Angeles.

Max noticed that while some actors used stage makeup, others used blends of flour, Vaseline, lard, and cornstarch. It was a hot mess—literally. Some actors' makeup would melt right off under the stage lights. In 1914, he invented "flexible greasepaint," a formula that launched a beauty empire. He kept the likes of Rudolph Valentino, Jean Harlow, and Judy Garland looking their best, and his company remains one of the biggest names in makeup to this day.

Hollywood made makeup mainstream—and not just for its starlets, but for the rest of the population who wanted to look like one. The flapper style also popularized makeup, with dark eyeshadow, red lipstick, and red nail polish. By 1925, the cosmetics industry was bringing in one billion dollars a year. Yes, makeup can make a pretty penny, but around this time, it was war that helped the industry get to that level of income.

The start of World War I marked a change in America's perception of makeup. With all these men away and the women learning how to do things like work in factories, the powers that be worried that everyone would just become a lesbian. So they promoted makeup as a way to maintain social norms. (I'm pretty sure that the housewives and sweaty hot factory workers still had plenty of lesbian sex, though.)

Red Cross ads featured angelic women wearing red lipstick matching their uniforms. There was even a term called "war face," which referenced how stressed out one looked and insinuated you needed to head to the cosmetics department, stat. With all the husband material away in battle, cosmetics companies turned to patriotism to sell compacts. "Even if your social or professional life does not demand it, your patriotism demands that you keep your face bright and attractive so that you radiate optimism," read a Helena Rubinstein ad.

But don't judge these old-timers too much for giving in to the commodification of war and gender roles. Honestly, makeup also became more popular during the Great War as an act of rebellion. These were dark days. A lot of people died. Brothers, boyfriends, fiancés, and husbands just didn't come home. So what did young women do? Who took the blame? They blamed their daddies and their parents' whole shitty generation for getting involved in the mess. So they wore as much blush as they wanted to. During this time, makeup became more accessible and affordable, so more young folks could get their hands on it.

During World War II, makeup was also used to boost morale. But here's a fun fact that will get you feeling patriotic: apparently, Hitler hated makeup. What a sociopath! He even listed "no makeup" as a literal rule in a handbook he had at his country retreat. Lipstick was the mark of a badass. In a 1941 *Vogue* article, one American soldier wrote, "To look unattractive these days is downright morale-breaking and should be considered treason."[60] What? That's not misogynistic: it's hilarious, accurate, and fights fascism! As it always has, the divine feminine offered reassurance during hard times. It's only a shame that until recently, in America cis white women were the only ones permitted to play with it.

Glam Gossip

Here's some tea for you: apparently, the Cure's Robert Smith kept a red lipstick hanging on a string next to his door to use on his way out so he'd apply his goth glam with a simple swipe.[61]

Perfume

I believe in fragrance and its powers. Perfume is the magic potion that transforms a charming woman into an enchanting one.

—Dita Von Teese[62]

After I finish getting ready, I walk over to my perfume altar and spritz my signature scent of Byredo Rose Noir on my décolletage, wrists, and often between my thighs. Perfume is the final step of my getting-ready glamour ritual. With top notes of cardamom, grapefruit, red berries; heart notes of lily of the valley, rose, violet, and jasmine; and base notes of moss, musk, patchouli, and cistus labdanum, I enchant my lover who always takes notice of my smell. While Byredo Rose Noir is both of our favorites—and a great gender-neutral brand—I often switch it up, opting for a Dior, or my best friend Annabel Gat's fragrance, Annabel's Birthday Cake, created by perfumer Marissa Zappas. When I wear a new perfume, it's as if I become a whole new person without losing myself. After all, the most important base note is your skin. Different perfumes can smell differently on various people. The pH value of your skin, the acidity of your skin fats, your diet, and your hormone balance all influence how a perfume will smell on you.

When glamour witch and inclusive beauty maven Rihanna released her perfume, Fenty Eau de Parfum in 2021, it sold out in hours.[63] Naturally, Rihanna celebrated by having caviar for breakfast. "Magnolia and musk unite with tangerine, blueberry and hints of Bulgarian rose absolute, geranium and patchouli, to create a unique blend that expresses itself uniquely on each wearer for a one-of-a-kind scent that is all heart and pure soul," reads the scent's description. Perfume is a natural business move for Rihanna, who is known for smelling like a goddess. When asked what his favorite scent was, Lil Nas X famously answered "Rihanna."

Lil Nas X is a style icon in his own right and, through his own charm, made rap music a more inclusive space for queer folks. And, of course, he brought back Satanic panic with a delightful gay twist with his music video for the hit "Montero." But he's not the first man to appreciate a quality fragrance. Alexander the Great, a king of the ancient Greek kingdom of Macedon, adored perfume. Historians describe him the way people talk about Rihanna today. "A very pleasant odor exhaled from his skin," wrote the Greek biographer Plutarch. "There was a fragrance about his mouth and all his flesh, so that his garments were filled with it."[64]

During Alexander the Great's time of 356–323 BCE anything considered favorable to the love goddess Aphrodite was en vogue. This included cinnamon, frankincense, and myrrh—the latter two were also given to baby Jesus by the Three Kings, so these are some seriously heavenly scents. Furthermore, historians write that Alexander the Great would use scent like a glamour witch. He had preferred scents for relaxation, and others he used as a time machine to invoke youthful memories. His instructor Aristotle, the legendary philosopher, taught Alexander that an understanding of scent wasn't just religiously

advantageous. The king's appreciation for plants and their properties would also make him a great leader. If you've ever felt a boost of confidence after spritzing yourself before a date or company party—with Fenty Eau de Parfum or whatever your signature scent is—you can understand why.

Many animal scents, in particular earthly notes, are used in perfumery. Musk is a key ingredient in Rihanna's potion and a plethora of other perfumes. Real musk (don't worry—Rihanna's perfume uses synthetic musk and is cruelty-free) comes from a pouch on the abdomen of the male musk deer, which lives in the mountains of the Himalayan and Atlas ranges.

The fecal-smelling ambergris used mainly as a perfume fixative is a rare growth that's sometimes produced in the stomach of the male sperm whale from undigested cuttlefish. The whale eventually throws it up, and it washes ashore worth a fortune. It's like a big expensive pearl for perfumery. And civet, which is a bit pungent on its own but enhances floral scents, comes as a byproduct of the anal glands of the exotic civet cat, a creature related to the mongoose. In the wild, the glands help the animal do one of two things—fuck or fight. So we steal the civet's magick perfume pouch for the same reasons it exists naturally. After all, glamour magick is excellent for attracting mates or destroying enemies.

But before you start feeling guilty about your adoration of fragrances, know that today most perfumers use synthetic ingredients created in a lab to mimic scents such as musk or civet. In the past, writings on perfumes read like a hardcore spellbook. For instance, the 1555 French perfumer book *Les Secrets de Maistre Alexys* contains a passage on "How to make a woman beautiful forever." It reads: "Take a young raven from the nest; feed it on hard eggs for forty days, kill it, and then distill it with myrtle leaves, talc, and almond oil."[65]

Death or disfigurement is a common aspect of the ingredients in natural perfumes—even those from plants. Benzoin, a balsamic essence, is created with cruelty. It's not produced naturally, so workers wound the tree by cutting its bark. The secretion then spills like blood, and the resin is collected to create the perfume material. It smells like vanilla, but its primary purpose is its fixative properties. Even sandalwood is pretty goth. Distilled sandalwood was used in

Ceylon—an island now known as Sri Lanka—to embalm the corpses of princes in the ninth century. If that's not spooky enough, sandalwood acts like a vampire all on its own. The tree is a hemiparasite, which means that while it gets some of its food through photosynthesis, it obtains the rest by siphoning off nutrients from nearby trees using tentacle-like roots until the host slowly dies.

Witches often face ethical concerns regarding the use of plants for their fragrance and spiritual properties, such as the controversy regarding the over-harvesting of white sage. The plant—beloved by witches for its smell, cleansing, and protective properties—is sacred to Native American tribes. However, you can find it on Amazon and at Urban Outfitters these days. While the accessibility is convenient, mass production risks overharvesting and devastation to the plant's natural habitat.

Many witches find that the most powerful scents come from their bodies rather than a sketchy seller on Amazon. Early in my witch training, a mentor shared that she preferred to simply apply her vaginal fluids to her neck and wrists when looking to attract a lover. So whether you use pussy juice or semen in place of perfume, it's certainly one way to save money. But in eighteenth-century Europe, perfume was quite popular to *cover up* bodily stenches, as bathing was rather unpopular. Even Versailles simply reeked. The irony is that many perfume ingredients emulate fecal smells but become alluring when paired with florals. For example, indole, which is found in jasmine, tuberose, and orange flowers, is also found in feces.

Scent is as primal as it gets, and not just because we all secretly enjoy the smell of our farts. The first place our sense of smell is processed is in the limbic lobe, where sexual and emotional impulses also occur. So whether your signature scent is a high-end perfume, your own creation of diluted essential oil, or your come, the use of fragrance is a scientifically approved glamour spell.

Nails

I just wanted to tell you all that I went to this shitty place to get my nails done (manicure + color), and they told me NO because I'm a MAN. I don't know what to think, but it's very unfortunate. What year is it? Fucking 1960?

—Bad Bunny[66]

When Puerto Rican rapper Bad Bunny graced the cover of *Allure Magazine* in November of 2021, he wore a domino manicure.[67] By rocking a domino manicure, he paid tribute to his roots. Dominoes are major in Puerto Rican culture. It was also a stark contrast to artists such as Gwen Stefani, who culturally appropriated Mexican American chola culture in her 2005 "Luxurious" video.[68] She wears a wifebeater, thinly drawn eyebrows, and a plaid shirt with only the top button buttoned. Parts of the music video take place in a nail salon, where Stefani gets acrylics mimicking rituals that are not her own. Anyone can get acrylics, but show a little respect, Stef!

The support Bad Bunny received for integrating his Puerto Rican heritage into glamour was positive, not only for looking fabulous but for breaking down stereotypes of how men should wear their nails. Fellow rapper Machine Gun Kelly recently released his UN/DN line of nail polishes with a range of shades including "Twenty Five to Life," an orange-red, and "Mary Jane," a forest green.[69] While such aesthetic and business decisions are breaking down gender norms, modern-day rappers are hardly the first men to rock a manicure.[70]

The men of ancient Babylonia manicured and colored their nails with kohl, and long before Machine Gun Kelly, they also championed a variety of hues—and not because it sucks when someone copies your manicure, but because there were different classes for different colors. The upper echelons wore black, while the lower classes wore green. These Babylonian babes were extra as well: they made manicure tools from solid gold. Before a battle, not only would they paint their nails, but they'd tint their lips to match and curl their hair. It's all just war paint.

Cleopatra also painted her nails by dipping them in a bottle of kohl. Dark red was her favorite color as it gave the appearance that her fingers were stained with the blood of her enemies. Since we're all just animals, blood red will always be iconic. In the 1994 movie *Pulp Fiction*, Uma Thurman's character Mia Wallace had nails painted in Chanel's Rouge Noir ("Vamp"). The color is meant to look like dried blood. It's still one of the most popular colors the brand offers to this day.

A manicure can be a spell, especially using color magick. Both Cleopatra and Thurman's Mia Wallace wore bloodred to display their power. Perhaps you want a purple manicure to invoke eccentric creativity while you learn a new Prince song on the keyboard. A green or gold manicure can invoke abundance when you ask for a raise. A cupid-themed red and white manicure with an accent nail can signal to your partner that you're ready for marriage. They'll be staring at your ring finger and won't even know it. Head to the spell section to learn how to cast this engagement glamour spell.

Nails—not the kind on your fingers, but the ones used in construction and carpentry—are historically employed in jar spells, usually to hex someone.

You get a photo of your enemy, toss it in a jar, fill it up with vinegar, nails, and sometimes even feces, and wait for such pain to manifest itself through sympathetic magick. Feel free to try it, if you like, although spells that lift you up rather than put others down tend to work better. Your ex may feel more pain by seeing your joyful, cupid-themed manicure complete with a rock on one finger than if you put them in a jar. Manicures are Venusian and healthily vain, but from a form of war paint to inciting jealousy, they also tend to serve a purpose.

Perhaps the most famous manicure, the French manicure, was created for pure convenience. In the mid-1970s, film directors were tired of starlets getting a new manicure every time they changed their outfits. Jeff Pink, the founder of the professional nail brand ORLY, was tasked with creating a glamorous look and cutting away the need for multiple manicures. "I got one gallon of white polish for the tips, and pink, beige, or rose for the nail," he told *The National* in 2014. Pink came up with the name "French manicure" on a flight to Los Angeles. The French manicure is just marketing at its worst and a glamour spell at its best. "The director commented that I should get an Oscar for saving the industry so much money," Pink said.[71] The fashion industry adopted the look for its versatility, and it's been a staple ever since.

But today, thanks to advances in nail technology, you can wear a French manicure or forest green hue in various ways. Long gone are the days of dipping fingers in kohl. Check out the list below to learn about the many ways one can style their talons.

Natural

Glam: It's best for your nails and goes with everything.

Sham: No offense, but life is short. Don't you want to do something with those nails?!

Regular Nail Polish

Glam: You can change it frequently and it won't fuck up your nails.

Sham: They say a regular manicure can last three to five days, but I always fuck mine up in three to five minutes.

Acrylic

Glam: Not only do acrylic nails last longer than gels, but they are also less expensive.

Sham: You need patience to sit through an acrylic manicure. Because they are filled in about once every two weeks, some people get bored with their color selection. They are highly glamorous but can damage your nails over time.

Extensions

Glam: Having talons makes you feel like a witch.

Sham: Be careful when working with orifices.

Gel

Glam: Gel can refer to a form of extensions that is similar to acrylic, but is more natural. It can also simply mean gel polish, which takes even less time than a regular manicure because you don't have to let them dry. They're basically bulletproof, so for people like me who can't paint their own nails, it's a wonderful option.

Sham: Gel extensions can be more expensive than acrylics, and also damage your nails.

Glamour Gossip

Acrylic nails—although glam as can be—have a rather unglam origin story. Where do they come from? The dentist's office. In 1957, dentist Frederick Slack broke a nail. As someone with tooth-fixing supplies, he repaired it using aluminum foil and dental acrylic from his lab. It made a nail so realistic that he had his brother produce and patent what we now know as acrylic nails. Wait, is the glamour trick on us?

Body Modifications

Pain feels good when caused by sexuality and vanity. So what's the common thread here? Consent. Body modifications—with the aid of a tattoo artist, plastic surgeon, or any other form of magician—can offer you a chance to defy genetics and your mother and have the nose or titties you've always wanted. In recent years and largely thanks to social media, the stigma surrounding plastic surgery has been declining. Today, beauty icons like Dolly Parton are getting honest about their work. "It is true that I look artificial, but I believe that I'm totally real," Parton told CBS in 2019. "My look is really based on a country girl's idea of glam. I wasn't naturally pretty, so I make the most of anything I've got."[72] Now, most of us would likely beg to differ: she's always been beautiful. But making the most of anything you've got is Glamour 101. The queen admitted to breast implants, a brow lift, and eyelid surgery. So you go, girl, and thank you for helping to normalize such interests. One could say the same about witchcraft and the bold #witchesofinstagram and TikTok sharing their spells and tarot insights with the world.

The United States boasts the most plastic surgery, followed by Brazil and China. Yes, body modifications can cause unrealistic beauty standards, but everyone has a right to do what they want with their own body. While witches understand the power of secrecy—and don't worry: if you get work done, there's no pressure to livestream the process—opening up about getting cosmetic procedures can also help lower unrealistic beauty standards. It's easier not to be jealous about Kylie Jenner's lips if you know that they're fake. And, as you'll learn, from the goddess Lakshmi's piercings through ancient mummies bearing tattoos of the holy Eye of Horus to the healing power of gender affirmation surgeries, spirituality and body modifications are bloodily and beautifully intertwined.

Botox

I'm against Botox.

—Melania Trump[73]

Botox is the most popular cosmetic procedure in the United States. There were over 2.5 million Botox injections in 2020, even in the midst of a pandemic. And let me tell you, as someone that gets Botox, it's not a big deal. It's like losing your virginity. Once you do, you'll wonder why you didn't do it sooner, and you'll want to keep doing it for the rest of your life.

Botox was FDA approved in 2002 for cosmetic use on frown lines. Botox, aka botulinum toxin, injected under facial wrinkles causes relaxation of those muscles, which smooths out the face. Botulinum toxins are some of the most poisonous substances known to humankind. But it's also supersafe as a beauty treatment when done by the right person.[74] Nightshade can be deadly, but that hasn't stopped witches throughout history from using it safely in flying ointment to harness its hallucinogenic (magickal) properties. Just don't bargain shop or use Groupon for Botox. Not only does this raise health concerns, but some places will dilute the Botox, which means it doesn't last as long. Anyone who is a licensed physician can administer Botox, but that doesn't make them the best person for the job. Go to a top-tier plastic surgeon or dermatologist. Botox is magick, but you want a good magician.

Getting Botox is like joining a secret society. Once you have it, you'll listen to people thank their "miracle eye cream" for the sudden disappearance of their wrinkles and have the satisfaction of knowing that they're lying. There's only so much that face creams can do. They don't penetrate the skin far enough. For another analogy, getting Botox is like going to the dentist, except it hurts less, is glamorous, takes a fragment of the time, and will likely cost less. I'm not suggesting that you sleep on your dental care, but hopefully, that helps put the experience in perspective.

While going to a private plastic surgeon's office makes for a rare glamorous yet medical experience—thanks, American health care!—the cost is a consideration for Botox. According to the American Society of Plastic Surgeons, the average cost of an injection procedure was $408 in 2019. Don't expect it to be a onetime payment either, because it only lasts about three months. If you like the results, you have to go back. If the idea of it just freaks you out, just don't get it. There's no right way to age, and one day we must stop judging people's personal decisions about their money, health, and body. Either wear your marks of time with grace or just find a plastic surgeon.

Botox takes about three to five days to kick in, with the ultimate results one week after injection. So, if you're getting it for an event, do it at least a week beforehand. Don't expect to walk out of the office and head straight to the full moon party. You probably won't look any more sprite yet, but you will possibly have bruising at the injection site. Don't worry. It's just from the needle, not from the Botox. The bruising goes away, and you can joyfully celebrate the results in a few days.

One of the most cited reasons to get Botox is to get a leg up at the office. Simon Cowell famously said that getting Botox added a decade to his on-screen career. It's the future. No one cares anymore. Just do what you want. Botox can also treat migraines, eye twitches, and excessive sweating, but this book is about glamour, darling.

Fillers

Thank God for puberty and fillers.
—Nikkie de Jager aka NikkieTutorials[75]

In the early 1990s, we filled syringes with collagen derived from cows. Today, it's just hyaluronic acid, a sugar-based gel. Think of fillers as just another sweet magickal tool in your arsenal, much like anointing your lips with honey to make your words sweeter. While cosmetic fillers such as Juvederm are usually hyaluronic acid, others, such as Radiesse, are made of calcium hydroxylapatite, which is a mineral-like compound found naturally in human bones. It improves the volume in areas of facial wasting that happen to HIV-positive people taking certain medications.

Cosmetically speaking, fillers can create a stronger chin or plump out dark undereye circles. They're also used to treat acne scars. And, of course, there's the infamous lip filler. As we age, our lips lose fullness. So it's only natural to want to get them plumped up! People still get their lips done, but today the filler is capable of much more. In conjunction, the use of Botox and fillers can recreate the effects of a nose job or a facelift or simply work in tandem to make your face look like you've never missed a night of sleep in your life.

The great thing about fillers is that your plastic surgeon or dermatologist can quickly reverse the effects if you don't like them. They're much easier to undo than a hex! But just like Botox, the biggest problem is that you'll love them. Honestly, get fillers while you can. Filler can make people in their fifties or sixties look overdone or even older. When we get older, our facial fat reduces, and we can start to droop. At a certain point, you just need a facelift.

Plastic Surgery

Life goes by fast. Enjoy it. Calm down. It's all funny. Next.
Everyone gets so upset about the wrong things.

—Joan Rivers[76]

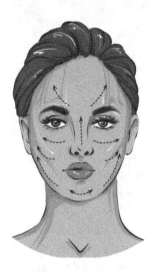

The word *facelift* invokes images of botched jobs on celebrity gossip sites. But when done correctly by a reputable plastic surgeon, it's not only transformative but will also save you money in the long run. The cost and time spent coming in for Botox and fillers for a decade will add up to more than one facelift. The same is true for filler rhinoplasties: they save you from going under the knife, but the effect wears off after a few months to a year. If you want something permanent and lower-maintenance in the long run, opt for a rhinoplasty. There's a common saying that "plastic surgery should whisper, not scream," but honestly, I've always had a soft spot for death metal. A knife cuts skin like a sword through earth. The goal is glamour. Plastic surgery is as witchy as it gets.

Nose jobs date as far back as the sixth century BCE when the Indian physician Sushruta outlined his forehead flap method for rebuilding noses. He performed this procedure on patients who'd lost their noses as a form of criminal punishment. Oof. Talk about nonconsensual body modifications.

Joseph Constantine Carpue performed the first nose job in the Western world after spending twenty years studying local plastic surgery methods in India. The procedure was reconstructive work done on a British military officer who had lost his nose to mercury poisoning.

Like so much in the art of glamour, plastic surgery was shaped by sex. Sixteenth-century Europe was experiencing a massive syphilis outbreak. In case you didn't know, untreated syphilis could rot your nose off, so surgeons started reconstructive techniques. But, as noted by government-ordered nose removal and war-induced mercury poisoning, it's not just sex that influenced modern plastic surgery. It's also violence.

The father of modern plastic surgery, influenced by Carpue, is generally considered Sir Harold Gillies. Originally from New Zealand, the otolaryngologist relocated to London. He developed many modern facial surgery techniques in caring for soldiers suffering from disfiguring facial injuries during World War I. His cousin, Archibald McIndoe, helped improve plastic surgery techniques during World War II.

But it was in 1887, when the American otolaryngologist—aka an ENT, or ears, nose, and throat doctor—John Orlando Roe documented what most agree is the first modern cosmetic rhinoplasty. It was done on a patient who was suffering "emotional distress" stemming from a "pug nose"—they hadn't caught on to inclusive terminology back then. Meanwhile, in Berlin, Jewish surgeon Jacques Joseph used a similar method to reduce the size of noses in European Jewry. Now, everyone has the autonomy to make decisions about their own body. If a Jewish person wants a nose job, let them have it. But it is impossible not to mention the role of race in cosmetic procedures: a white pointy nose becomes a common goal of rhinoplasty; Cardi B praises her thick body, and skinny white girls want ass implants. Thankfully, today, any plastic surgeon worth your money will work to maintain your ethnic identity while still obtaining your goals.

For instance, double eyelid surgery is extremely popular in South Korea. While it's easy to jump to accusations that this is the result of white supremacy's effect on beauty standards, as David Yi points out in *Pretty Boys: Legendary Icons Who Redefined Beauty and How to Glow Up, Too*, the double eyelid aesthetic dates back to the 1896 Japan. An ophthalmologist named M. Mikamo created it. The *futae mabuta* are Japanese people with a natural double eyelid, so maybe not everything is about you, white people.[77]

While the rich were getting cosmetic surgery on the down-low for most of the twentieth century, procedures such as nose jobs and facelifts became available to the masses in the 1970s. By the 1980s, cosmetic procedures soared, particularly liposuction, matching the decade's fitness craze. But even before the facelift went mainstream, people were doing what they could to remain youthful, especially those in old Hollywood whose face was their moneymaker. The "Hollywood Lift" consisted of silk thread, rubber bands, paper tabs, and glue, which would lift and pull back the face, hidden beneath hair. And it wasn't just women getting work done; it never was. Even Gary Cooper had some help. But it's still pretty stigmatized for men—especially straight men—to undergo cosmetic procedures. As of 2018, men accounted for only 8 percent of plastic surgery patients.

The following are common plastic surgery procedures:

Facelift

Glam: Facelifts can last up to a decade. There are many facelifts, including a mini facelift, an S-lift, and even nonsurgical options using only Botox and fillers. The deep plane facelift lifts only under the muscle, leaving the skin attached, which avoids the stretched look that other facelifts can come with. Both the superficial musculoaponeurotic system (SMAS) facelift and deep plane facelifts target the lower two-thirds of the face. (Botox works much better on the top half of the face, such as around the eyes on the forehead.) Today, different facelift options finally address the different ways various ethnicities age.

Sham: It's expensive, there is recovery time, and some people prefer to age naturally.

Nose Job

Glam: With a well-done nose job, you'll never need to contour again. After rhinoplasty, you're likely to be happier with your overall appearance, as this one feature can transform your entire face.

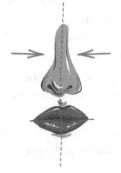

Chin filler can make your nose appear smaller, just as a nose job can help your chin appear more powerful.

Sham: We are finally moving away from a world where only one nose job is available: the pointy ski slope white girl nose. Many people want to maintain the ethnic characteristics of their noses when getting rhinoplasty, and now, at any reputable plastic surgeon's office, that's available to them. Nose jobs become harder to do with each revision, which is why it's essential to go with someone like Dr. Dara Liotta, aka the Nose Job Queen of New York.

Breast Implants

Glam: Big titties.

Sham: Both silicone and saline implants can rupture. Implants don't last forever; most people get theirs replaced every ten years. Consider the cost of maintenance before getting your boobs done.

Butt Implants

Glam: Butt implants include actual implants (much like for breasts) and fat grafting, aka the Brazilian butt lift, where a doctor transfers fat from another part of the body into the booty. You can also get both simultaneously for the most natural look possible. As Sir Mix-a-Lot said, it's all about the buns, hon!

Sham: Don't inject illegal silicone into your ass; it's really dangerous! Real talk: When skinny white girls get butt implants, it can look super fake, but maybe that's what they're going for. Like breast implants, silicone butt implants need to be replaced about once every ten years.

Liposuction

Glam: Liposuction removes unwanted fat and is sometimes referred to with the much more glamorous name of body contouring.

Sham: Liposuction doesn't improve cellulite dimpling or remove stretch marks.

Vaginal Rejuvenation

Glam: Vaginal rejuvenations include labiaplasty and other procedures to alter a pussy. (And I use that to include the vagina, labia, mons, and clitoral hood, all of which you can get surgery for.) It's probably the most controversial plastic surgery because people assume societal-ingrained self-consciousness drives people to get it. Still, frankly, I think that robs one of their bodily autonomy. You can do whatever you want with your pussy.

Sham: Your pussy really is beautiful the way it is.

Penis Enlargement Surgery

Glam: It's your body, and society needs to stop shaming men for their dick size. Body shaming isn't cool regardless of who is on the receiving end.

Sham: Studies on the safety and effectiveness of penis enlargement procedures are a bit spotty, and the most one can reasonably expect to gain is an inch in length.

Gender Affirmation Surgery

The work begins by each of us recognizing that cis people are not more valuable or legitimate and that trans people who blend as cis are not more valuable or legitimate. We must recognize, discuss, and dismantle this hierarchy that polices bodies and values certain ones over others.

—Janet Mock[78]

Gender affirmation surgery refers to procedures that trans or gender nonconforming folks get to match how they feel inside with how they look on the outside. While the U.S. continues to be fraught with transphobia, that wasn't always the case in North America.[79] Remember, Indigenous two-spirit people are considered sacred and often act as balance keepers and healers within their communities. However, such folks are still at high risk for hate crimes—both for their gender and race. According to the Human Rights Campaign, at least fifty transgender or gender nonconforming people were fatally shot or killed by other violent means in 2021.[80] The Nazis are still here, and it's a witch's duty to be ready to punch them at all times. But, to start, let's learn about how glamour can help make GNC people happier and healthier.

Gender dysphoria is the distress that can happen when your sex assigned at birth does not match your gender identity. Procedures that address this include facial surgery, top surgery, and bottom surgery. Nonsurgical options include hormone therapy, puberty blockers, and voice therapy. Finally, gender euphoria is the joy and contentedness one experiences when how you feel on the inside does match how you look on the outside.

According to the Cleveland Clinic, about one in four trans and nonbinary people opt for gender affirmation surgery.[81] While it should be every trans person's right to have safe and affordable access to such procedures, it's important to note that we shouldn't expect it. Whether the cost is an issue or whether one feels better as is, we should always respect someone's gender identity. For many, changing their name and pronouns will do. What someone's junk looks like is, frankly, none of your business.

Even when someone does want gender affirmation surgery and is ready to pay for it, it's not always easy. We still give trans and nonbinary folks a whole lot of ridiculous hoops to jump through. For example, most insurance companies require one to submit documents before covering a gender-affirming surgery, such as health records that show a history of gender dysphoria and a letter from a psychiatrist. Conversely, there isn't a sound, reliable system in place to help them navigate healing from the procedure and other issues that come with being a trans person, such as the massive underemployment and discrimination they face.

While being GNC or trans is certainly not an illness, research does show that gender affirmation surgery can be good for one's mental health. For example, one study found that the odds of needing mental health care went down by 8 percent each year after the gender-affirming procedure.

Surgical procedure options for those assigned male at birth include:

+ Facial feminization surgery

+ Adam's apple reduction

+ Breast augmentation

+ Removal of the penis and scrotum (penectomy and orchiectomy)

+ Construction of a vagina and labia (feminizing genitoplasty)

Surgical procedure options for those assigned female at birth include:

+ Facial masculinization surgery

+ Breast reduction or mastectomy

+ Removal of the ovaries and uterus (oophorectomy and hysterectomy)

+ Construction of a penis and scrotum (metoidioplasty, phalloplasty, and scrotoplasty)

Dora "Dörchen" Richter (1891–1933), of Germany, is the first person to undergo complete male to female gender affirmation surgery. She acted and presented as a woman from when she was a child. At six, Dora was already experiencing so much gender dysphoria that she tried to remove her penis with a tourniquet. After being arrested multiple times for cross-dressing, she received special permission from the police to wear women's clothing. In 1931, Dora became the first woman to undergo bottom surgery. She lived and worked at Berlin's Institute for Sexual Research during the 1920s and early 1930s. After the Nazis took over, in May of 1933, a gang attacked the institute. It's assumed that Dora died at their hands. Remember, witches, work on that lead hook.

Tattoos

I used to self-mutilate—I'm bipolar and manic depressive—so I've been getting happy tattoos over my scars, not to cover them completely, but to remember that I don't have to take it to that place if I feel sad. A fan wrote that it gave her hope; that she wanted to be alive. Comments like that make transparency so worth it.

—Brooke Candy to *The Face*[82]

Let's give credit where credit is due. The best tattoo shop was in Polynesia, as detailed in the logs from the voyage of Captain Cook in 1769, although he doesn't get the credit. Polynesians were the best at tattooing in the ancient world, and we still wear their designs today. They often used elaborate geometric designs, which were added throughout your life, so your tattoos grew with you. Think of it as sacred geometry on the skin.

Another great place to get inked was Egypt. One of the seven 3,000-year-old mummies discovered at Deir el-Medina, a village in ancient Egypt known for its artisans—a woman—had roughly thirty tattoos. Most notably, these included the hieroglyph *nefer* meaning "to do good" and the Eye of Horus, a magickal symbol that brings protection. From Lady Gaga's peace sign tattoo to

Justin Bieber's "Son of God" chest piece, people continue to use body modifications as spiritual armor.

While Bieber and his insane collection of Jesus tattoos prove the pop star doesn't think ink is a sin, historically, Christians judged the hell out of people for having tattoos. When the Spaniards saw tattoos on locals as they landed on the coast of Mexico in 1519, they assumed they were works of Satan. When today Samoan body art is appropriated, Christian missionaries in the 1800s tried to get the Samoans to stop, telling them, "Tattooing is numbered among the works of darkness and is abandoned wherever Christianity is received."[83] However, Christians did help end the practice of tattooing slaves and criminals as the religion spread through the Roman Empire—although focusing on ending slavery itself probably would have been better. Early Christianity was built on slaves. While white folks may have gone around preaching about how sinful tattoos are, they weren't above using them as a gruesome currency. For example, in New Zealand, European traders would trade a musket for a local Maori tattooed head.

The Christians tried to stop tattooing by turning it into a sin. The Byzantine emperor Theophilus (812–842), however, weaponized tattoos into straight revenge. Two monks who dared criticize him were tattooed on the forehead with obscene iambic pentameter under his order. The rebellious and criminals have been forced to get tattoos as punishment throughout history. But the tattooed have also been punished to a life of slavery for their tattoos. In September of 1691, a South Sea Islander covered in tats was nonconsensually brought to London to be exhibited as a freak. His name was Prince Gigolo. He died shortly after his arrival of smallpox.

In the eighteenth century in a continuation of their function as protection spells, tattoos became good luck charms among the sailors who wore them. Sailors are strange and unusual. It's just the cost of life on the sea. They also were sailing to foreign places such as Polynesia, so they were turned on to body mod trends earlier than the rest—and had the balls to get them. Sailors during the world wars inspired a large amount of the U.S. tattoo industry, and Sailor Jerry (1911–1973) and his sailor-style tattoos continue to influence the tattoo industry today.

While stick and pokes are all the rage today and you can count on any Scorpio to have one, for a tattoo that lasts opt for the machine. Samuel O'Reilly, a New Yorker, invented the first tattoo machine in 1890. Modern tattoo machines use electromagnetic coils that move an armature bar with a barred needle up and down into the skin. In the book *Tattoo: Secrets of a Strange Art*, Albert Parry wrote, "The very process is essentially sexual. There are the long, sharp needles. There is the liquid poured onto the pricked skin. There are two participants of the act, one active, the other passive. There is the curious marriage of pleasure and pain."[84] Tattoo artists are professionals, but giving and receiving a tattoo is highly intimate. I've reported for *VICE* on couples that get off on tattooing one another.

I also have a neck tattoo of a weed leaf that I got when I was very stoned at SXSW to celebrate my first book deal about cannabis. Tattoo regret happens and has always happened. The ancient Egyptians practiced tattoo removal using a mixture of lime, gypsum, sodium carbonate, pepper, rue, and honey. My advice? Unless you have a hate symbol tattooed on you, lean into your old bad tattoos. What's the other option: to live in shame? A glamour witch would never!

Of course, tattoo removal options are available, but they are not an eraser, as doctors continuously warn. Black ink comes off the easiest. Blue, yellow, and green tones are harder to remove. Some places claim they can remove everything using a new technology called PicoSure, so we can assume tattoo removal will become a more refined process. It is trickier on dark skin, but even if you're snowy white, you can expect to go back for two and half years on average, once every three months. Unfortunately, you must wait between sessions because the tattoo removal process is a bit of a gnarly procedure. Each time the tattoo is lasered, particles are broken down and digested by your immune system. Then your skin blisters before healing over. The regeneration period takes up to eight weeks. And then you do it again!

Not only is it complicated, but tattoo removal is also expensive. The American Society for Aesthetic Plastic Surgery estimates the average cost per session at $463.[85] It's painful as well, although if you can handle a tattoo, you can probably handle a removal. Unfortunately, the better your ink, the more difficult it is to remove. That stick and poke that you let your green-haired crush do on your forearm after the first date? That should be no problem to take off.

If you're not up for two and a half years of expensive laser treatment, you can get the old tattoo lightened just enough for a cover-up. And suppose you ever need to temporarily hide your tattoos for important moments like meeting the parents or posing for your sex worker social media account? In that case, Dermablend makes body makeup that provides fantastic temporary coverage.

I've added a few tattoos to change their meaning, but I find an old tattoo worn with confidence much sexier than a faded "I tried to remove this" semi-lousy tattoo. Tattoos can act as markers or talismans, which show our growth like rings on a tree. As an ancient Samoan song shares, "Your necklace may break. The *fau*-tree may burst, but my tattooing is indestructible. It is an ever-lasting gem that you will take to your grave."

Piercing

There are a multitude of reasons for getting pierced, from the superficial to the profound. It might be all about expressing independence, attracting attention, the sensation of metal through flesh, or the opportunity to wear some gorgeous jewelry.

—Elayne Angel[86]

If you think septum piercings are a new trend, you couldn't be more wrong. The oldest body jewelry, dating back to 4400 BCE, is believed to be a septum piercing found in Australia. The jewelry was made of bone, which is still a favorite adornment material among witches who shop on Etsy. While animal parts in spells are undesirable for some witches, fangs can be used for protection, and the raccoon baculum, or penis bone, is used in spells to attract sexual attention.[87]

One would integrate a penis bone into their witchcraft for reasons similar to getting their penis pierced. Piercings have consistently shown that you are tough, ready for battle, and can take pain. Not only was 5,300-year-old Ötzi the Iceman found with many tattoos, but he had every parent's nightmare: stretched earlobes.

Piercings also show your status in society. This can refer to a social class, whether you're a punk living in a squat house or a suburban mother who wants a diamond in her nostril. With the rise of luxury piercing jewelry, the body modifications that used to show rebellion and anarchy are now a way to signal your wealth. But piercings have always had a pretty side. In the Vedas, India's ancient religious texts from around 1500 BCE, the goddess Lakshmi wore earlobe and

nose piercings. Gold jewelry from the fifth century created for pierced ears was found by archaeologists in the tomb of the Ukok Princess on the border of China and Russia—and she also had a rad tattoo sleeve). The Ukok Princess, whose mummy was discovered in 1993, was also known as the Siberian Ice Maiden and believed to be an essential guardian against evil powers. The locals were not happy about her body's removal, and so in 2012, the mummy was returned to her home of Altai, now a Russian republic in southern Siberia.[88]

While a piercing can indicate that you're everything from a crust punk to a Park Avenue cougar, it can also serve a healing purpose or as a form of harm reduction. "Some people seek piercing to distract themselves from stress and difficult times or circumvent the desire to self-harm," writes Elayne Angel in *The Piercing Bible*. If you are considering self-harm, please see a mental health professional before a piercer, but there's spiritual honor in finding healthy methods, such as safe piercing, to experience pain. Getting pierced can be a sacred ritual even for those who just enjoy the sensation or do so for explicitly religious purposes. In Central Australia, shamans of Aboriginal tribes wore tongue piercings that had the diameter of a pinkie finger. They believed that if the hole closed up, their shamanic power would be lost.

Piercing can also function as an expression of sacred sexuality. The word *thrill* comes from the Middle Eastern term *thrillen*, which means "to perforate by a pointed instrument; hence, to cause a shivering, throbbing, tingling, or exquisite sensation; to pierce; to penetrate." In Japan some particularly fashionable yakuza were stylishly ahead of their time and would insert pearls under the skin of the penis. Pearling is still done by yakuza today, often in prison, with one pearl for each year served.[89]

But using jewelry as a form of erogenous zone body modification is even carried out by prudish types. The Victorians—infamous for finding makeup and nail polish offensive—saw a nipple piercing craze, according to Stephen Kern, who wrote 1975's *Anatomy and Destiny.* "In the late 1890s, the 'bosom ring' came into fashion briefly and sold in expensive Parisian jewelry shops. These 'anneaux de sein' were inserted through the nipple, and some women wore one on either side linked with a delicate chain. The rings enlarged the breasts and kept them in a state of constant excitation.... The medical community was outraged by these cosmetic procedures, for they represented a rejection of traditional conceptions of the purpose of a woman's body," he writes.[90] You never know who has a secret genital piercing until their clothes come off.

The BDSM scene heavily influenced piercing culture. Gay S&M kids led by Doug Malloy birthed modern-day piercing, becoming culturally notable in the 1980s. At the time, there was just one shop. Gauntlet opened on Santa Monica Boulevard on November 17, 1978 (a Scorpio!). Shaman, artist, master piercer, and body modifier Fakir Musafar coined the term *modern primitives* in the 1980s to describe the connection between body modification and the spiritual use of piercing and to remind us that trends are never really trends, only repeated expressions of human behavior. Musafar was born in 1930 on South Dakota tribal land and died in 2018, leaving a legacy for his impact on body art and modification.[91] He found early support from the gay and bondage scenes simply because they understood what it was to be different. "We were all excluded from regular society, so we had something in common," he told a documentary for French television. "We were fighting for a common goal, and that was to be let alone, to be able to do what we wanted to do, not be thrown into mental institutions, harassed, bothered by authorities."[92]

One of the most excellent current uses of piercings is gender expression. Modern-day trendy piercing studios, such as Studs, see this and frequently feature gender nonconforming influencers in their promotional efforts in lieu of your standard cis agency model often found in jewelry campaigns. Piercing can be a way for trans and nonbinary folks to connect with their bodies. If you're on hormone replacement therapy, wait at least two years to get a piercing so that the tissue can change. Also, wait at least one year for scar tissue to form after getting genital gender confirmation surgery.

While we're on the liberal agenda: practice gun control, and don't use piercing guns! They are inaccurate and can even carry blood-borne pathogens from previous clients. While a piercing done with a needle allows the jewelry to be slid through with precision, guns shoot an earring right through the tissue. There's no room for various size lobes, infection is riskier, and frankly, they are just out of style.

Let's look at the popular piercings.

Ears

Lobe

Glam: Even if someone has no other body modifications, they're likely to have a lobe piercing. It's an easy and fast healer that will accommodate lots of jewelry.

Sham: The lobe is kind of like the gateway drug of piercings. If your lobe is big enough, you can get additional lobe piercings, but soon you might have to move up to the cartilage.

Helix

Glam: The helix refers to the upper cartilage of the ear. You can wear hoops in this area—although most places pierce with studs. If you get pierced in the midsection, it's called a flat. You can get multiple piercings in this area and other parts of your ear cartilage to form your own couture ear. The forward helix is the upper fold of cartilage near your scalp.

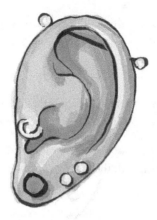

Sham: You have to earn your piercings. If you're used to the month-long healing time of a lobe, get ready for the possibility of a year with no sleeping on one side.

Rook

Glam: The rook sits in the inner cartilage, above the daith and between the inner conch and the forward helix. It is usually pierced with a barbell. The faux rook allows one to wear a flat back piece of jewelry that comes in from behind the ear rather than through the rook itself.

Sham: Expect at least a year to heal this guy.

Daith

Glam: The daith is a piercing on the cartilage adjacent to the face, below the rook. You can wear gorgeous circle barbells in this piercing. Daith rhymes with "moth" and comes from the Hebrew word *da'at*, meaning "knowledge."

Sham: Recently, people are after this piercing to heal migraines because it's supposed to be an acupuncture region, but it doesn't work.

The daith actually goes through the acupuncture points for the mouth and butthole, so it's more of a sex thing. Get it because it looks pretty.

Tragus

Glam: The tragus is that small cute little fold of cartilage where your face turns into your ear. It's just begging to be adorned with sparkles!

Sham: You can't wear earbuds while this is healing, so if that's how you get your music, stick with the helix.

Conch

Glam: The conch is done in the inner ear, in the deep round center. There's enough canvas there for more than one piercing.

Sham: You also can't wear earbuds or earplugs while the conch is healing. Sorry music lovers.

Industrial

Glam: An industrial piercing refers to two piercings held together by a single bar, usually in the helix area. It looks metal AF!

Sham: If healing two piercings held together by a giant barbell sounds tricky, that's because it is.

Face

Eyebrow

Glam: This piercing indicates that you are not to be fucked with.

Sham: I didn't say that was a good thing.

Nostril

Glam: A small sparkle can add dramatic flair to your nose.

Sham: Be careful of your jewelry when you blow your nose.

Septum

Glam: Septum piercings have been cool for thousands of years, back when tribal people wore a bone through the spot. Today, septum rings are the perfect sexy hipster look.

Sham: In case you needed a reason not to snort too many bad drugs, having a deviated septum can make it trickier to pierce.

Lip

Glam: Bring attention to that sexy pout. Lip piercings can resemble a beauty mark, as labret piercings, and more.

Sham: As with the tongue, lip piercings can cause dental issues, so either prepare to practice perfect dental hygiene or stick with lipstick.

Tongue

Glam: Everyone wants the kid with the tongue ring to go down on them.

Sham: You can seriously cause dental damage with a tongue ring, and they've largely fallen out of fashion as a result.

Torso

Nipple

Glam: Having your nipples pierced gives you power that one must experience to understand.

Sham: Getting your nipple pierced really does hurt. While it can enhance sexual pleasure, you also need everyone to stay away from it for at least six months. Get one at a time so that your lover can suck the other nipple.

Navel

Glam: The navel piercing is sexy on all bellies.

Sham: You may need a break from sit-ups for a few weeks, but of course, this could be considered a plus.

Genitals

VCH (Vertical Clitoral Hood)

Glam: An actual piercing of the clitoris is rarely recommended, so mostly what you see is a vertical clitoral hood piercing.

Sham: The VCH piercing closes right away when you remove the jewelry, so unless you want to get pierced again, wear pretty jewelry that your love. It's what your pussy deserves.

The Princess Diana

Glam: The Princess Diana is the same as a VCH, except they go to the side(s) of the hood instead of the center. The piercing was named after the first woman Elayne Angel performed it on, and this was also an era in which Diana was in the news at times—not to mention, piercers seem to get off on naming things after British royalty.

Sham: Not everyone's pussy is built for this piercing.

Outer Labia

Glam: You can use your labia piercings like a corset to hold up your stockings.

Sham: Be ready for healing time and be sure that you want permanent holes in your labia. Also, it can bleed for a week after healing.

Inner Labia

Glam: This area is pretty easy to heal.

Sham: It also doesn't provide much sexual stimulation, which is the point of most genital piercings.

The Prince Albert

Glam: The Prince Albert is an infamous piercing that's placed through the skin at the tip of the penis. While it looks intense, less tissue is actually used than in a love piercing. It's also known for providing sexual stimulation for all parties.

Sham: There is a decent amount of bleeding that occurs after getting a Prince Albert. Don't be alarmed.

The Frenum

Glam: The frenum piercing is a bar that goes along the underside, or frenum, of the penis. You can get one, or many go for ladders. Yes, they are good for sex. They take a regular penis and make it ribbed.

Sham: These can leave scar tissue when taken out.

Others

Corset Piercings

Glam: Corset piercings which are made on the back using rings and ribbons. They look quite pretty.

Sham: It's a painful process that is impossible to heal, so it's a temporary look often done for events and photo shoots.

Dermal Piercings

Glam: Dermal piercings go under the skin and can add a sparkle to the neckline, wrist, or your area of choice.

Sham: They can also fall out after just three months, so mind your diamond jewelry.

PART TWO

Glamour Grimoire

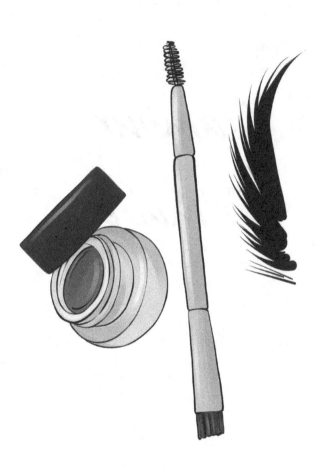

4

GLAMOUR FOR BEAUTY

There's nothing wrong with looking nice. Cleopatra loved her milk and honey face masks without shame, like a queen, and so should you. That's why we're going to make one, along with using tarot cards to find the right hair color for you. Beauty is about looking as fabulous on the outside as you feel on the inside. However, thanks to society—which continues to focus its celebrations on white, sample size, able bodies—it's more than understandable that sometimes we need the help of witchcraft to feel our best. But times are changing, which is why you can use this chapter to freeze away Botox fears or embrace your inner crone. These spells show you that self-care and beauty rituals work in reverse. Sometimes, glamour rituals like working with ancestors can begin with our skin and soak into our souls. And remember witch: you are in control.

What Hair Color Is Best for You? A Tarot Spread

You will need: Your tarot cards, your hands, a mirror

The best time to cast the spell: Whenever you're considering switching up your aura

Glamour witch says: Today, thanks to both high-end salons and affordable options at home—companies like Manic Panic and Overtone make affordable semipermanent fun color options—you can change your hair to every color of the rainbow. While traditional advice suggests considering your skin tone, that doesn't mean that any color is off-limits. For instance, whether it is a highlighter hot pink or a blush tone, there's a pink for everyone. The color magick section explains that pink conjures self-love, sweetness, or punk rock femininity. From blue to brown, every color has a unique vibe that you can use to express yourself. So now that you know that you can wear any color you like, what shade should you try next? Let's ask the cards.

The Spell

1. First, let's double-check your skin tone. Take a look at your veins. While the skin on your arms can change seasonally due to the sun, the area on your wrists reliably show your vein color. If they look blue or purple, you're probably cool-toned. But if your veins are green, you likely have a warm undertone. Another test is to hold up your favorite shirt to your face. If it's blue, green, or purple, that implies a cool skin tone. On the other hand, you likely have a warm skin tone if you look best in yellow, reds, and oranges. And, if you're one of the lucky ones who look great in everything, then your skin tone is neutral—or you're a mighty glamour witch!

2. Remember, regardless of your skin tone, there is a shade of green, or even blonde, for everyone. The main question is: What vibe do I want to give off? Pull a card. Sometimes, such as after a breakup, we may wish for a bold look. Other times, something more natural is desirable, perhaps because it's easier to maintain. What did you draw? For instance, let's say you pulled the Ace of Cups. This loving card of creativity and intuition asks you to open your heart to love, especially self-love. If you want to take a more literal interpretation of the water flowing from the cup, this could indicate that pink is right for you, or even blue. The magick of tarot is that it doesn't tell you the answers. Instead, the cards reveal what you already know.

3. Pull another card, this time thinking about the logistics rather than the color. Is money a concern? Do you want something easy to maintain, or are you OK with regular touch-ups at the salon? Do you want a low-key change, such as highlights or a total baby blonde to goth black makeover? Pull a card. Let's say that you pulled Strength. The Strength card is all about courage, being in control, and channeling animal instincts in a constructive manner—which is what self-expression through glamour is all about. In this example, the card is saying go big or go home when it comes to your new look. You know that hair color that you've always wanted to try but were scared to pull off? Guess what? You can totally pull it off.

4. Finally, stand in front of a mirror, and hold the two cards on either side of your face. This gives you a visual to pull both skin tone considerations and magickal desires together. In my example, using the RWS deck, both the Ace of Cups and Strength card contain yellow, which is not the best for my cool undertones. If I want a red, I'll likely go for something rich rather than on the yellow-orange spectrum. Also, seeing these power cards next to my face reminds me that I'm a bad enough witch to pull a bold red off.

5. Now that you know what color you want, go ahead and book your hair appointment or buy your supplies if you're working at home.

Milk and Honey Cleopatra Face Mask

You will need: An apron, ½ cup honey, ½ whole milk, a whisk, and a bowl

The best time to cast the spell: When you want to feel as pretty as a queen

Glamour witch says: Cleopatra was ahead of her time when it came to beauty and is primarily known for her honey-infused milk baths. Today, we know that milk contains lactic acid, an alpha hydroxy acid that can improve skin tone and texture. Likewise, honey can help open pores and, because of its antibacterial properties, can also treat breakouts. Throughout this book, you'll notice the magickal use of honey in other ways, too. For instance, witches often apply honey to their lips to sweeten their words, and it's also used in candle spells as an offering to the gods and to help attract nectarous abundance. But, in this spell, these two magickal ingredients are here to help your skin.

The Spell

1. Put on an apron, get out your honey, milk, whisk, and bowl. You're a kitchen witch, now.

2. Mix equal parts (½ a cup works well) milk and honey until a thick mixture forms.

3. Apply the mask to your face. Let it sit for fifteen to twenty minutes.

4. Gently scrub off using your hands or a soft towel.

Glamour Magick with Ancestors

You will need: A pen and paper, a computer, DNA ancestry test (optional)

The best time to cast the spell: Whenever you feel called, although Scorpio season is particularly powerful for communicating with the ancestors

Glamour witch says: Some people find glamour inspiration from connecting with their ancestors. In particular, marginalized folks, such as Black Americans and Indigenous people, can find great power in reconnecting with their ancestral roots and embodying that through clothing and hairstyles. It's also a reminder that cultural appropriation can rob people of this experience, so save the feather headdresses for Native Americans and locs for Black Americans.

Others do not relate to our ancestors. Maybe you come from an abusive home filled with violence with a history to match. Fuck those people. You're related to far more folks than you know. For instance, after getting a genetic test done, I discovered that I have roots in Scotland. Are there any other *Highlander* fans here? I was already dyeing my hair ginger, so the natural next step was to learn about the witchcraft practices from Scotland. It's the country where the word *glamour* originated, after all!

You'll connect with trusted ancestors in this spell and then create a digital glamour altar inspired by them.

The Spell

1. To start, be honest with yourself. Do you feel an urge to connect with your ancestors, perhaps even a recently deceased family member? Or do you have a problematic relationship with your blood relatives? If the latter is the case or you simply want to know more about your lineage, consider using a DNA ancestry test to learn more about your heritage.

2. Once you have the information, whether it's from your grandmother or online research stemming from your genetics test, take a moment to meditate on your findings. What about your ancestors do you wish to include in your current glamour routine? Perhaps you want to wear braids like your great-grandmother or, if you recently discovered you have Scottish roots, give tartan a chance.

3. First, let's get analog. Write a letter to your ancestors. Convey why you need them and how you wish to carry on their legacy through glamour. Fold up the letter and place it on your glamour altar.

4. Now that you know what you want, let's go digital. Set up an online mood board using Pinterest or other social media tools. Begin researching the glamour traditions of your ancestors. Pin up images of clothing, hairstyles, skin care rituals, and whatever else inspires you.

5. Whenever you feel uninspired or lost, look to the board to beautifully get in touch with yourself with a dose of ancestral protection.

Sacred Pain with Piercing

Trigger Warning (TW): Self-harm

You will need: A printer, pens (ideally metallic), a quality local piercer

The best time to cast the spell: When you're craving a new piercing

Glamour witch says: Piercing can allow one to experience pain in a sacred and delightfully vain manner, in the same consensual way BDSM and kink can. Pain is not always bad. From Native American suspension practices to Krishna's pierced ears, piercing and body modifications continuously appear in rituals and worship worldwide. (Of course, if you have any thoughts about self-harm, please tell a mental health professional immediately. Call the National Alliance on Mental Illness at 800-950-NAMI, or 911 for an emergency.[93])

On a more fun and frivolous note, who doesn't love a reason to wear more jewelry? Today, there are piercing shops with safe, pretty, and affordable services. Follow this ritual to experience consensual and sacred pain while adorning your nose, nipple, or even genitals—head to the Piercing section of this book for a rundown on piercing placement options—with sparkling jewelry.

The Spell

1. First, you need to decide what you want to have pierced. Perhaps you already know that you need a navel ring, or maybe you're curious about cartilage piercings. Using your phone, take a photo of your ear, genitalia, or entire naked body and print it out.

2. Using pens—ideally metallic ones to mimic piercing jewelry—draw some piercings on yourself. Play around and do your research. When you're at the piercing studio, your piercer can speak to which will work best for your unique anatomy.

3. Schedule an appointment at your local piercer. Make sure to do your research and read reviews to ensure you go somewhere safe, reputable, and within your budget.

4. After you pick your piercing location and jewelry and your piercer has a needle in hand, focus your entire mind on how beautiful you'll look in your new jewelry. There will be a lightning-quick pinch, but all that's on your mind is how dope your nipple will look wearing a rose gold barbell. Notice how you can overcome pain with the power of your mind.

Make sure to follow the aftercare instructions your piercer gives you.

Plastic Surgery Plant Medicine Recovery Remedy

You will need: ⅛ ounce of cannabis, a nonstick baking sheet, parchment paper, a hand grinder, one cup water, one stick of unsalted butter, a medium-size pot, a mason jar, cheesecloth

The best time to cast the spell: While recovering from plastic surgery, a piercing, or whenever you need some delicious pain relief

Glamour witch says: After getting work done, you need to rest and let your body heal. Your doctor likely prescribed you pain medication, which you should take as directed. However, if you need a little extra relief or prefer plant-based medicines, cannabis contains pain-relieving and anti-inflammatory properties, which can help you heal faster. It's ill-advised to smoke after surgery, but an enhanced treat might make your recovery even more relaxing.

Occult history is fraught with the use of cannabis. For instance, one tradition recalls witches sprinkling hemp seeds while circling a church nine times to summon love. You may have heard of cannabis's inclusion in the infamous Flying Ointment, an herbal blend including other psychoactive and sometimes poisonous plants such as opium poppies, datura, belladonna, and nightshade. Allegedly, witches would smear it on their broomsticks—likely a euphemism for dildos—blast off like a high priestess.[94]

Make your cannabis-infused butter ahead of time, or have a friend do it while you lounge on the couch. You can then add it to your favorite baked treats or even a savory dish. While cannabis is very safe, always consult your doctor before taking any herbal supplements.

The Spell

1. Procure your plant medicine. Whisper to the buds, "Help me heal and transform into the next incarnation of my beautiful self."

2. Preheat your oven to 240°F.

3. Cover a nonstick baking sheet with parchment paper and scatter your eighth of cannabis onto it.

4. Bake for thirty to forty-five minutes or until golden brown. This process is called decarboxylation. Cannabis produces a nonpsychoactive acidic cannabinoid called THCA. When we smoke or vape, the heat converts THCA into THC, which does have euphoric and pain-relieving effects. If you don't decarb your cannabis, you're going to have some weak-ass weed butter, and no witch wants that.

5. Take the cannabis out of the oven and let it cool.

6. When it's ready, grind it up. Use a hand grinder, which you can get at a dispensary or kitchen supply store.

7. Mix one cup of water and one stick of butter in your pot. It should simmer until the mixture is smooth and melted.

8. Stir in the decarbed cannabis. Continue to let the medicine simmer for two to three hours, being mindful not to let it boil.

9. Cool your concoction and strain the cannabutter into a mason jar through a cheesecloth.

10. Place it in the refrigerator and let it cool.

11. Now you can use your magick butter in place of Muggle butter to make cookies, top spaghetti, or whatever you desire. Remember to practice responsible dosing. Try starting with a quarter teaspoon, and see how you feel after an hour. Increase dosage as needed.

12. Relax, enjoy, and heal.[95]

Freeze Away Your Botox Fears

You will need: Pen and paper, a cup or ice tray, water, your freezer

The best time to cast the spell: When you want to get Botox—or any work done—but are worried about others judging you

Glamour witch says: As detailed in this book's plastic surgery section, getting Botox is no big deal when done by a top-notch plastic surgeon or dermatologist. Depending on how much you get, there's a quick pinch or two, and you're done within fifteen minutes. Warning: You will like it and want to keep coming back. It does work. But despite how commonplace and accessible Botox is these days, there's stigma around the procedure. If the only thing holding you back is fear of rude people's judgment, you need to act like a witch and freeze them before they accuse you of freezing your face.

Witches often freeze their enemies. These spells aren't exactly hexes, but more like disarming someone so they can't hurt you. So let's freeze anyone who might give you a hard time—and your own fears while we're at it.

The Spell

1. Take a moment to meditate. Do you really want Botox? If so, what is holding you back? Are you worried a partner, family member, or jealous friend may judge you? Or are all the mean voices in your head coming from your insecurities? If you don't actually want Botox, this is also a critical moment to reflect on and realize that.

2. On a small piece of paper, write down the name of anyone who might be talking smack. But frankly, most of the time, our fears around getting what we want can stem from our inner critic. Rather than someone's name, you can write down what you're worried about. For instance, you may want to write, "I might look fake" (you'll be fine!).

3. Fold up the piece of paper, and place it in a cup or ice tray. Fill the cup or ice tray with water, making sure you leave some room at the top since ice takes up more volume than the same amount of water. Then, put it in your freezer. Your haters and insecurities can no longer hurt you.

4. Get your injectables, witch. When you feel comfortable and secure enough in your fabulous face, you can take your friends and fears out of the freezer.

Call upon the Crone (Glamour for Aging Spell)

You will need: A fresh pomegranate, ⅓ cup plain coconut yogurt, one tablespoon honey, one teaspoon lemon juice

The best time to cast the spell: Whenever the ageist ills of society are getting to you and you want to feel beautiful

Glamour witch says: Pomegranates are associated with Persephone, the gorgeously devious Queen of the Underworld. She was always one step ahead of her cheating husband Hades by transforming whatever nymph he was chasing into a tree or some other plant. Of course, you don't need to transform potential side pieces into trees, and you deserve better than a partner who requires you to do so. But we can learn from this glamorous albeit jealous goddess. While topicals can't stop wrinkles, there are still so many fantastic remedies for your skin, and pomegranates, which are rich in vitamin C, are one of them. According to plastic surgeon Andrew Jacono, MD, FACS, pomegranate oil can play a significant role in collagen synthesis, which helps reduce the appearance of fine lines and wrinkles. More research suggests that pomegranates can help reverse UVA- and UVB-induced skin damage in humans and even support DNA repair.[96] And you can save money, bust out your kitchen witch skills, and make your own! Many magickal ingredients are lost along the way through processing in commercial beauty products containing pomegranate oil.

The Spell

1. Break open a pomegranate. Whisper into the seeds, "Let's feel beautiful, Persephone." You can alter your language, but give the girl some credit!

2. Measure out roughly a third of a cup of seeds. Pop them in the blender with the rest of the ingredients, strain, and transfer to a clean container.

3. Wash and dry your face and apply directly to your skin.

4. Let the mask sit for fifteen to twenty minutes, or whenever it starts to dry.

5. Gently rinse off.

5

GLAMOUR FOR MONEY
AND CONFIDENCE

Once again, for the witches in the back: Save the financial guilt for the billion-aires. You deserve to do what you love and make a decent profit, which is why we're going to perform a ritual to upgrade your relationship with money, mate-rial girl. But we are witches, and witches love animals and the beautiful plants that produce so many beauty ingredients. So we're also going to glamorously go green with a vintage séance. We'll invoke the sun for the perfect selfie and even summon the romantic poet Lord Byron to burn away body shame. Your ticket to bigger checks and higher self-esteem is confidence, so let's brew some up.

Fake It Till You Make It Luck Potion

You will need: A travel-size bottle of your favorite perfume, one eyelash, sage

The best time to cast the spell: When you're ready to increase your professional confidence and level up in the world

Glamour witch says: Dress for the job you want, not the job that you have. In this vain world, it works. Sometimes we want to slip away unnoticed. For instance, in addition to protecting against COVID-19, face masks are an excellent disguise when paired with sweatpants to prevent your ex from recognizing you at the pharmacy refilling your meds. But this chapter isn't about evading the paparazzi; it's about becoming so successful that they know who you are.

As discussed in the perfume section, perfume is a scientifically approved glamour spell. The first place our sense of smell is processed is in the limbic lobe, where sexual and emotional impulses also occur. So not only will a small amount of perfume give you confidence, but its allure spreads outward to others. Yes, this can help us attract mates, but the spell works on anyone you seek to influence. Because perfume can wear off between four and six hours[97] and you never know when you might run into a professional connection, it's best to keep some on hand—with a secret magickal ingredient, of course. The lore surrounding making a wish on an eyelash before blowing it away is believed to come from the nineteenth century. Blowing it away from you keeps the devil away. But, in today's world, the devil wears Prada. So let's use perfumes—i.e., potions—to help you feel your best professionally.[98]

The Spell

1. Anyone with Sephora Beauty Insider Points knows how easy it is to get perfume samples. They come in such cute little bottles and are perfect for this spell. So start collecting them. Any department store will also have them. When you get one that makes you feel like the most powerful, Nine of Pentacles rich bitch—and, yes, that's a gender-neutral term—out there, hold on to it.

2. Luscious eyelashes transform your face. They are all you need to feel hot. Not only are eyelashes—whether enhanced by makeup, extensions, or

falsies—beauty must-haves, but those sweet tiny hairs are also magickal. So the next time one falls off, whether natural or extension, save it. Try to pick one that's not slathered in mascara.

3. Quickly run your perfume sample bottle through sage smoke to clear any negative energies collected.

4. Hold your eyelash. Make a wish. It can be anything from "I wish I make six figures next year" to "I wish to turn my side gig into a full-time business." Pro tip: The universe knows much more than we do, so sometimes it's OK to keep a wish general.

5. Carefully, making sure not to spill any precious potion, unscrew the top of the perfume.

6. Gently plop the eyelash into the perfume bottle. Rescrew the lid.

7. Keep it in your purse or bag at all times. Use it before any major professional meetings.

P.S. Yes, honey. This spell will work on lovers, too. Just try not to shit where you eat!

Vintage Green Glamour Séance

You will need: Six white candles, sage, your vintage clothing, cannabis (optional)

The best time to cast the spell: Ideally, cast this spell at night when the moon is in Scorpio. Scorpio is the sign of death, rebirth, and transformation. It's also ruled by Pluto, the Lord of the Underworld. So it's an ideal time to communicate with the dead.

Glamour witch says: If you're worried about the environment, buying vintage is a great way to skip around new production. It can be expensive, but you can also find treasures in vintage shops, and the shopping experience is such a treat. A great place to find deals on vintage is eBay, but you have to hunt around. Used clothes and jewelry can feel powerful as if they carry the magick of each glamour witch who wore it before you. For example, I have my grandma's 1950s nightgown and sleep in it when I feel scared and need protection. And let's be honest: vintage fur is just more ethical than new fur.

If your vintage item is from a stranger, you may want to get to know them. And, if you get bad vibes, you may want to cleanse it with sage in addition to regular washing—following the care directions, of course, since vintage is delicate. So let's have a séance to see what we're dealing with for the sake of saving our planet while looking fabulous.

The Spell

1. Find a lovely space, about six feet in diameter, where you can get comfortable. Place the white candles in a circle. Sage the entire area.

2. Begin facing east, and light the candles clockwise until you end up facing north. You have cast a circle and are now protected.

3. Sit in the middle of the circle holding your vintage item.

4. If you partake in cannabis, feel free to light up a joint or take a hit of your vape. For some witches, cannabis can sharpen intuitive abilities.

5. Close your eyes. Take several rounds of deep breaths. Say out loud: "Thanks for the swag; all queens are drag. I'm a witch in the present, and I love your style. Do you wish to tell me anything about yourself and your mercantile?"

6. Listen. Are you holding a sweater purchased after a heartbreak? A vest someone wore to their first job?

7. Stay in the circle until you feel satisfied. Use your newly downloaded information on your apparel's previous owner to inspire you, and continue to be conscious of your fashion choices concerning the past and present.

8. If you get any evil vibes, give it away. But a little sage and dry-cleaning should do the trick if you just can't part with it!

Summon Your Alter Ego

You will need: A human figure candle, a power playlist, sage or another cleansing herb bundle, matches or a lighter, a pen and paper, candle-carving tools

The best time to cast the spell: The full moon, which is a primal time of manifestation

Glamour witch says: Your alter ego is just you minus the insecurities. We have to hear every insecure thought. No one else can see those intrusive thoughts as long as you hold a confident posture and a calm gaze.

Just like Lady Gaga or Frank Ocean, creating a new name for yourself can help you become the person you were always meant to be. There are chosen families, so why not chosen names? If you're using it for social media, there's also the added security of not having all your legally accurate information out there. But you don't need to create a new name to have an alter ego; you just need one you can step into like a magick cape. Beyoncé had Sasha Fierce for when she's nervous about performing. So who can you turn into when you need to weaponize confidence? Let's use your brainpower and a candle spell to find out.

The Spell

1. Find somewhere quiet to set up. Gather your supplies. You'll need a human figure candle, which you can buy online or at your local occult store. Choose whichever one resonates best with your gender. And, if you don't want to use a human shape, a regular candle will do.

2. Put on your power playlist. This is one you've filled with the music of artists who make you proud to be you.

3. Sage yourself, your candle, and your candle-carving supplies.

4. Take your time, listen to the music, and write down words that evoke confidence—such as *fierce*. Words have power; casting an incantation is simply this. Your alter ego will be a spell—one that you can step into whenever you're worried other people can see the anxious voices in your head.

5. Look at what you've written, and pick a name for your alter ego. Go with your first instinct!

6. Carve the name into your candle. It's OK if it's messy. Work over newspaper or a trash bag to make cleaning up easy.

7. When you're finished, set your candle on your altar. Light it up. When the candle stops burning, the spell is complete.

8. Whenever you doubt yourself, remember the name of your alter ego, and step into that confidence like it's armor—because it is!

Sun Ritual for the Perfect Selfie

You will need: A well-lit room with a view of the sun, your phone

The best time to cast the spell: The few hours after sunrise or before sunset, known as "the golden hour," is the best time for portrait lighting. But any time of day will do. Sometimes a selfie simply can't wait.

Glamour witch says: An Instagram filter is a glamour. And before filters, there was photoshopping, and before photoshopping, there was literal airbrushing. Before that, the rich requested of their portrait artists to minimize a large nose and maximize their jewels. But whether it's a selfie or even a painting, you need good lighting to look good. And that means making friends with the sun.

In witchcraft, the sun is associated with the divine masculine. Think of Billy Porter at the 2019 Met Gala, dressed in gold as a "Sun God," and carried on a chariot by six chiseled men. The sun represents boldness, authority, and action. Conversely, the nurturing and mysterious moon, associated with the divine feminine, represents intuition and the wild unknown. So, regardless of our gender, we all contain the masculine and feminine of solar and lunar energy. But, to take the perfect selfie, you'll need to connect with the sun.

The Spell

1. After getting yourself selfie-ready, take a moment to sit somewhere in your home facing the sun. Close your eyes and open your palms to receive the sun's light. Feel its warmth. Imagine the sun's rays filling you up with gold glitter.

2. While seated, chant: "I am powerful, I am hot." Just like the sun, you are. Repeat until you feel strong and confident.

3. When you're ready, take out your phone and get into your selfie pose. Turn toward the sun. Natural light from a window is ideal, or use a ring light which mimics that effect. Backlit photos rarely look good unless you're going for that glowy feel.

4. If you're using your arm, extend it outward and upward. Then tilt the phone toward you, turn your face at a three-quarter angle, and snap away.

5. When you're finished, thank the sun. Not only does it provide you with excellent selfie lighting, but the world revolves around it.

Here are some additional tips for taking the perfect selfie:

- Consider investing in toys. A selfie stick is just another magick wand. Just like a good vibrator can make your sex life better, a ring light and a selfie stick can upgrade your selfie game.

- Take a ton of photos. Take hundreds if you want! Kylie Jenner famously says she takes "like 500" before finding one she wants. I find it easy to scroll through my selfies and favorite ones that I like. Then I delete the rest, so I don't use up all the space on my phone.

- Filter that photo to hell, bitch. Utilize all weapons and assume your enemies are doing the same. Not only can the right app slap on a chic filter, but you can do things like add sparkles or a flower crown to make your selfie match how you feel inside. What is the line of too much editing? Your Tinder date needs to recognize you in person! Filters are just virtual makeup.

- Experiment, experiment, and experiment. Only you know your best angles, and only you can learn them through trial and error.

- Be mindful of your background. For example, make sure that you don't accidentally include your boyfriend's college copy of *Atlas Shrugged* that's on your bookshelf.

- Experiment with both vertical (portrait) and horizontal (landscape) formats. Some people look better doing it horizontally!

- Selfies are another reminder that posture matters. Stand up straight and stick out your neck to avoid double chins.

- Hold the phone above and out for bigger eyes, and then bring it in toward you.

- Use your hands! A hand in a selfie can make it so much cuter. Throw a peace sign, a sign of the horns, or just some hair touching.

+ While I'm OK with duck face, you may not be. So opt for a kiss face instead of anything birdlike.

Upgrade Your Relationship with Money, Material Girl

You will need: Sage or other cleansing herbs, matches or a lighter, honey, a green candle (a pullout seven-day candle if possible), money-drawing incense, a coaster, newspaper or tissue paper (so you don't make a mess!), candle-carving tools (available online—toothpicks or a knife also work, but be careful!), money-drawing oil, gold or green glitter (optional)

The best time to cast the spell: Friday, which is ruled by Venus, the goddess of love, beauty, and abundance

Glamour witch says: Madonna said it best: Experience makes you rich. We live in a history-making era where society is questioning this horror show of an economic system we call capitalism. It's exciting to see young witches form unions and press politicians. Still, I want to make something very, very clear: Being critical of wealth distribution does not mean that you should feel guilty about money, honey! Save some of that shame for the billionaires!

If you've ever stuck an affirming sticky note to your desk, such as "I make six figures a year"—you may not, but it ushers in the right vibes—then a money candle isn't all that different. It's a powerful ritual to remind yourself of your worth and then get that dough. All materials required can be purchased online or at your local occult shop.

The Spell

1. Light your sage and blow the smoke over yourself, your candle, and your candle supplies.

2. Sit quietly and meditate. Visualize yourself as a wealthy glamour witch. Perhaps there is a specific monetary figure you have in mind. Visualize that, too.

3. Take a taste of honey. You must make sure it's not poisonous before you offer it to the gods! Then, if you're using a pullout candle, squeeze some in the bottom to help attract money with the sweet nectar—and help keep the candle stuck in place. (But don't put the candle back in the holder yet: there is more to do first.)

4. Light your incense. Let the smoke billow all over your green candle. If you're using a pullout candle, let the incense fill up the glass holder. Place a flat object such as a coaster on top to keep the smoke in.

5. Over newspaper or tissue, carve a big-ass dollar sign into the green candle. If you're after a specific figure, feel free to add that too. Carve your name and zodiac symbol into the candle as well.

6. Anoint the candle with fragrant money oil.

7. If it pleases you, roll the candle in glitter. I suggest using gold (which represents the abundance of the sun) or green (for money and health) for this spell. Shake the glitter in a straight line on the newspaper or tissue paper, and then roll the candle in it.

8. Remove the coaster from your candle and plop the candle inside the smoky container. Light it up!

9. Keep the candle somewhere near your desk so that you can see it while you work. When it's finished, the spell is complete.

P.S. Now, I can teach you how to make a money candle, but I am not an economist and can't instruct you on how to make a budget. However, Tiffany Aliche, aka "The Budgetnista," can. I can't recommend her book *Get Good With Money* enough.[99] So now say this incantation with me one more time: I deserve money, and I will make it.

Love Your Tattoos

You will need: Tumbled rose quartz, fragrance-free lotion

The best time to cast the spell: Daily, ideally right after you bathe or shower

Glamour witch says: As anyone with ink can attest, it's not uncommon to have a complicated relationship with your tattoos. If you genuinely dislike your tattoo or made the mistake of getting something that you now understand to be offensive, see the tattoo section of this book to learn about removal options. However, let's assume that you generally like your ink and want to keep your tattoos well cared for. Not only will this spell keep your tattoos moisturized—which helps the ink last—but the self-love properties of rose quartz remind you that it's endearing to have a peace sign on your ass that you got at age eighteen. This spell is for healed tattoos. Always consult your artist about proper aftercare—which usually involves a few days of Aquaphor followed by unscented lotion—whenever you get new work done.

The Spell

1. Make sure that you have a tumbled piece of rose quartz. Tumbling smooths out all the rough edges. The pink crystal represents sweet self-love.

2. Keep an unscented bottle of body lotion, such as Aveeno, handy.

3. After you get out of the shower or bath, or whenever your skin feels dry or your tattoos could use a little love, apply some lotion onto your adorned skin. Then use the smooth rose quartz as a massage stone to rub the cream into your inked skin. While you do so, whisper to your tattoos, "I love you, I love you, I love you."

Lord Byron Body Shame Banishing Spell

TW: Body dysmorphia

You will need: Four pieces of clothing whose tags you don't mind cutting off, scissors, a cauldron or other fireproof container, matches or a lighter

The best time to cast the spell: During the waning moon phase

Glamour witch says: When you're buying clothes, the only thing that matters is that they make you feel and look good. However, with a fashion industry that has only recently started to include bodies of all sizes, it makes total sense that many of us hate the sizing stress that comes with shopping.

Lord Byron, perhaps the most romantic poet of all time, experienced body dysmorphia. In case you haven't heard, the guy was the sexiest thing Europe had ever seen, and he broke the hearts of all genders. Seriously, this guy looked like an even more refined version of Harry Styles. However, he was born with a right clubfoot and bullied as a child. As his fame grew, he put himself on strict diets. Remember, during his time, homosexuality was still punishable by death in England, so when word of his pansexual love affairs gained traction, he fled the country. After joining the Greek War of Independence, Byron died in Greece at the age of thirty-six from a fever contracted after the First and Second Siege of Missolonghi. He's considered a wartime folk hero just as much as a romantic revolutionary.

For us—and the tragic poet—we're going to burn away body shame with an incantation by Byron himself.

The Spell

1. Pick four clothing items whose tags you are OK with cutting out. Sizing changes with time and varies significantly from designer to designer. You want to buy clothes because they look good, not based on a number.

2. Take your scissors and snip out the tag without damaging the clothing. Place them in your cauldron or firesafe container. In tarot, the number four is associated with calm and confident manifestation.

3. Go somewhere spacious so that you can practice fire safety. Get out your lighter or match.

4. Light it up. While the tags burn, chant four times a lovely line from Lord Byron's *Four Longer Poems*: "Love will find a way through paths where wolves fear to prey."

5. When the fire is safely out, dispose of the ashes. If you live near nature, you can bury the ashes away from your home. However, if you're a city witch or simply too tired to leave the house, throwing them in the garbage is perfectly fine.

6

GLAMOUR FOR LOVE AND GENDER

Before society uses your sexuality against you, read this section to use your sexuality to get ahead in society—and learn to love yourself while you're at it.

Are witches temptresses who use their looks and wit as tools of seduction? Yes, but that's not a bad thing. You deserve a love that honors you and to express your gender as you see fit. That's why, in addition to injecting witchcraft into the breakup haircut ritual, we're going to harness the power of the moon to charge your strap-on. Likewise, there's a manicure spell for marriage for witches interested in getting engaged, and for genderqueer witches looking to party, get ready to summon Dionysus. Of course, you can adapt all of these spells to your unique orientation, relationship format, and gender.

Post-Breakup Haircut and Cord-Cutting Ritual

If she changes her hair after a breakup . . .
she's gone forever, Bruh . . . new hair . . . new man . . . new life.
—Internet meme[100]

You will need: A professional hairdresser, sage, matches or a lighter, Florida Water or another cleansing tool, a black candle, black cotton thread or yarn, scissors, and a cauldron or firesafe container

The best time to cast the spell: Wait two weeks to a month after a breakup—or as long as you need to process it and be able to get a haircut without making any despair-fueled poor style choices you'll regret later. While this spell works whenever you need it, a new moon is ideal for fresh starts. However, if you can, avoid making significant changes to your appearance if Venus is retrograde.

Glamour witch says: The breakup haircut is a mourning tradition that allows for healing and rebirth. Native tribes let their hair grow very long and only cut it during mourning. And make no mistake: a breakup is a time of mourning. Acknowledging that helps you allow yourself to mourn. Breakup haircuts not only let you mark a transformation but also separate yourself from the past. Cutting your hair also literally snips away pieces of you that your former lover touched.

Cord-cutting is a form of sympathetic magick that allows you to sever ties with a person or relationship which no longer serves you. It's the magickal version of getting rid of split ends. Perform this cord-cutting ritual, then get your actual split ends snipped off, and get ready to debut a fabulous new look for your ex to drool over on Instagram.

The Spell

1. First, take some time to mourn. The first days, weeks, or even months—depending on the relationship—can be a chaotic time. It's OK if you're not totally over the breakup, but you want to feel stable enough to make a haircut choice you won't regret later. Use the first week or so to process your emotions and create a Pinterest board of haircuts you like. It's always best to show up at the salon armed with photos, so your hairstylist knows precisely what look you want.

2. Book your hair appointment. Take it from someone who once went to the emergency room after trying to cut my own bangs: it's best to leave beauty rituals that require sharp objects to the professionals.

3. Perform the cord-cutting ritual the night before your appointment. Open your windows to release the negative energy your ex left behind and ensure that your fire alarm doesn't go off from any smoke from the spell. Sage your home, spritz it with Florida Water, or whatever your favorite witchy cleansing method is.

4. Light your black candle. Perform a round of clearing breaths: Inhale for four. Hold for four. Exhale for four. Hold for four. Witch each cycle of breaths, visualize releasing your pain. Repeat until you feel calm.

5. Sit cross-legged and use your black thread or yarn to tie your ankles together. This represents your former lover and the pain holding you back. Keep your scissors nearby!

6. Loosely bind your wrists together as well.

7. Take a few moments to meditate on the relationship. First, let yourself feel the loss. Then, when you're ready, chant three times, "I release myself from the pain of the past."

8. Pick up the scissors and snip both your wrists and ankles free.

9. Place the discarded black cord in your cauldron or firesafe container. Light it on fire and let it burn away, taking your pain with it.

10. If you live somewhere with outdoor space, bury the ashes as far away from your home as you can. But, if you're a city witch or just tight for time, it's perfectly fine to throw them in the garbage. Just make sure nothing is still burning. Witches must know fire safety.

11. Get a good night's sleep, wake up, and go to your hair appointment feeling like the star that you are.

12. After your appointment is over, make sure that your stylist takes plenty of pics. Post them on IG. Not only will you attract new lovers, but you can be sure that your ex is stalking your account and will see them and feel jealous.

Use the Moon to Charm Your Strap-On

You will need: Your strap-on dildo, a pen and paper, sage, any favorite crystals

The best time to cast the spell: The new moon

Glamour witch says: Anyone can have a dick. Don't let cis men get cocky. With a few clicks on your computer or a visit to your local sex shop, you can have a dick too, vulva-owners. Strap-on dildos are where fashion meets function. You can have an average-size dick, a giant purple monster dick, or a sparkle dick that vibrates. But before you wear it, it's helpful to charge your dick by infusing it with the power of the moon. The dark new moon is a time for fresh starts and intention setting. Use this spell when you want to charge a dildo you just purchased or cleanse one after a breakup. While some people prefer tossing out sex toys after a breakup, dildos can be too expensive to throw away, and it's normal to form an emotional attachment with your cock—even if it's store-bought. And if you don't want to throw an old cock away but don't know what to do with it, dildos make great sculptures to place around your home. Miley Cyrus infamously decorates her house with sex toys; why can't you?

The Spell

1. Sitting somewhere comfortable with a view of the dark sky, meditate while holding the dick. What do you want it to bring you? Love? Sex? Concentrate on your desires.

2. Using your pen and paper, scribble down your intentions. You don't need perfect grammar or even complete sentences, but writing down spellwork helps you identify your needs and provides a log to refer to when it's time to perform a future spell.

3. Sage the cock by running it through the smoke.

4. Literally cleanse it by washing it with mild soap and water. You want a non-porous, body-safe silicone. Please don't go for cheap dildos; they can soak up germs and become impossible to clean.

5. Hold the dildo in your hands tightly while concentrating on everything you want. Visualize yourself feeling more comfortable in your gender, having great sex, or even wearing it for a kick-ass burlesque performance.

6. Place the dildo, sticking straight up, in view of the magickal dark sky. If you have favorite crystals, you can use them to form a circle around the dildo. Let it sit there overnight as your intentions infuse the strap-on.

Get Engaged (Mani for Marriage)

You will need: Quality nail polish and steady fingers or a good manicurist

The best time to cast the spell: When you want to be proposed to

Glamour witch says: If you want to marry your partner, perhaps all they need is a little manicure charm utilizing color magick. Marriage isn't for everyone and wasn't even legally available to all orientations until recently. However, it is not only romantic but sacred to commit yourself to your partner through a ceremony. Please only use this spell if you're turned on by the idea of being married to your partner and not just in it for the ring and party.

An accent nail is simply a manicure with one finger different from the rest. For this spell, we are using the ring finger. The example

I'll use is a red manicure with a pink heart added to the ring finger, but please adjust for your taste and color magick needs. Oh, and in case you were hoping, yes, this spell includes sex magick.

The Spell

1. Pick out your magick manicure. I go with classic red nails—red represents passionate love—with a teeny pink heart accent for sweet love added to my ring fingers. You may prefer to opt for a gold accent nail if you want a gold engagement ring and joy, so refer to the color magick section to learn what's best for you.

2. Do your nails, or visit your local nail salon. (Don't forget to tip!)

3. Take some time to meditate on what your dream wedding looks like. Visualization is crucial, especially in sex magick, so get a clear picture. Is it big? Small? What are you wearing? What expression of love is on your future spouse's face?

4. Keep marriage on your mind while wearing the manicure. Touch your lover's face, inspect your nails while hanging out, and get your partner to notice them.

5. Practice sex magick, which simply means harnessing the power of your orgasm for manifestation. Use your hand during sex to have an orgasm. Some witches prefer to practice sex magick solo, even when in a relationship. For one thing, it can feel more ethical, and for another, there are fewer distractions. And for a third thing, you can easily use your magick manicure to get off if you're masturbating.

6. While you bring yourself to orgasms, fantasize about your partner. Think about your hottest sexual fantasy, anything involving them, but at the moment of orgasm, visualize your dream wedding. Come your face off.

7. Modern witches understand that spells pair best with therapist-approved communication. If you're grown-up enough to practice sex magick, you should be able to enjoy a relaxed conversation about marriage with your partner.

Glamour Magick for Dating Apps

You will need: A pen and paper, a selfie-ready look, your phone and dating apps

The best time to cast the spell: On a Friday, which is the day of the week the goddess of love Venus rules

Glamour witch says: Dating apps are miraculous; they can introduce you to an abundance of partners you might not cross paths with in real life. But let's be honest. They're also a pain in your hot little ass. Most of the "glamour magick" we see today on dating apps comes from filters, and it's OK to use retouching apps—everyone else is. So do enhance what you have, but don't make yourself unrecognizable. Ideally, the goal is for them to see you in person. However, because we're witches, we're going to add a secret sigil to your profile to help you attract the best partner.

The Spell

1. First, put your phone away and take out a pen and paper. Write a paragraph detailing what you want out of your mobile dating experience. Be honest and specific, but allow enough room for the universe to bless you with surprises. After all, you never know who might be perfect for you.

2. Boil that paragraph down to one word. You're going to make a sigil.

3. Let's say that your word is *endgame*. On another piece of paper, create a magickal symbol—otherwise known as a sigil—using the letters in your

word. Pick out one letter from your word. For instance, for *endgame*, start with *e*. Draw an *e* shape on your paper. Cross out every *e* in your word.

4. Move into the next letter. Let's say that you pick *g* and draw a *g* around your *e*. There's no right way to make a sigil, and it's OK if it's messy. Continue until you are out of letters and have a cute personal dating app sigil.

5. Now, you may already have a dope dating profile. But regardless of if you need to start from scratch or update your photos, it's time to take a selfie.

6. Before you do, using your pen, draw the sigil onto your skin. Hide it under your clothes, so no one catches on. Perhaps place it over your heart or on your inner thigh.

7. Now take a sigil selfie. Upload it to your dating app. While you're at it, review your profile, or go ahead and make one. Remember to consider color magick. For instance, include purple to lure in a creative bisexual or blue for a tranquil relationship.

8. Start swiping! Because you're a modern witch, here are a few extra tips:

    +   Don't be afraid to message first. It's attractive. Some people literally swipe on everything and then filter from there, so you might need to stand out of the crowd.

    +   Additionally, don't be afraid to show off your accomplishments. If you went to SXSW, show yourself in front of that step and repeat—just not if your ex is also in the photo.

Learn to Accept Love

You will need: A rose quartz, a tarot deck, pink sticky notes, pink underwear

The best time to cast the spell: Friday, which is the day of the week ruled by lover planet Venus

Glamour witch says: Confidence is the core of glamour, but it can be hard to get to a place of such security, especially if you are a trauma survivor. If you didn't grow up feeling secure in love or have had your heart broken one too many times, it could be hard to trust the affection of others. However, until you realize how deserving you are, it's easy to self-sabotage opportunities for romance and all matters of abundance. Use color magick, crystals, and the iconic Empress card to cast a confidence spell to learn to accept love.

The Spell

1. Find somewhere comfortable to meditate, such as on a pillow or yoga mat in front of your altar or vanity. Place the rose quartz to your left. The sweet pink stone calls in kindness and self-love and helps attract the healthy attention of others.

2. Take out the Empress card from your tarot deck. The Empress represents abundance, beauty, and love. She works with all genders and reminds you that you are a goddess and love witch worthy of everything that you desire in this life. As Cassandra Snow writes in *Queering the Tarot*, "The Empress queered is gay or queer bars that are inclusive. The Empress queered is queer open mic nights where anything goes. The Empress queered is letting friends crash on your couch because they have nowhere else to go, buying your friend who doesn't have a job a coffee to perk them up, handing down your old clothes to someone who's transitioning."[101] The Empress is a loving mother who shows up. Place the Empress card to your right.

3. Close your eyes and take a few cycles of deep cleansing breaths. With each inhale, visualize inhaling a magical pink stream of shimmering love. With every exhale, release self-hatred and negativity. Visualize a toxic oil-like tar finally exiting your body. Continue until you begin to feel loved and calm.

4. Continue to carry your rose quartz with you. Many witches simply stick it in their pockets. Or, you can wear rose quartz jewelry.

5. To keep the Empress energy with you, place the tarot card (or a printed-out version to protect your deck) on your vanity, or tape it to your mirror. It's also helpful to change your phone wallpaper to the Empress card.

6. Finally, if you don't already own an epic pair of pink panties, consider treating yourself to some. If pink makes you uncomfortable, feel free to skip this step. But remember that stepping outside of your comfort zone is healthy, especially if it allows you to put a personal spin on powerful colors such as pink, which have been unfairly gendered over the years. Pink is the color of self-love, and wrapping your most delicate areas in pink satin is a beautiful use of color magick.

Celebrate Your Gender Identity with Dionysus

You will need: Your party playlist, a goblet (every witch should own an epic goblet), wine (or grape juice), your favorite makeup, a mirror

The best time to cast the spell: Before a night on the town

Glamour witch says: Dionysus is most famous for being the Greek god of wine. However, Dionysus would be fine with you calling him a goddess, too. According to legend, Dionysus was assigned male at birth but lived as a girl until adulthood. Then, he pretty much rejected any gender classification, living a fabulous bigender life. Dionysus's effeminate male presentation is believed to be why he intimidated other Greek gods and their uptight followers so much. Dionysus loves grapes, parties, and orgies; however, his main concern is you having a good time while looking and feeling like *you*.[102]

So let's call upon him to help you have an epic night out while celebrating your unique gender identity.

The Spell

1. Put on your party playlist.

2. Pour yourself a glass of wine, ideally into a ceremonial goblet. You can get a witchy goblet everywhere from Etsy, Renaissance Faires, or your local occult shop, although a wineglass will do. If you don't drink, grape juice works just fine. But, honestly, pour some seltzer if you prefer: Dionysus only cares that you're happy and having fun.

3. Before you take a sip, bless your wine. Whisper into the goblet: "I call upon Dionysus, a down-ass god, whose rejection of gender norms we applaud. I wish to party, but as my true self: bless this wine with sexy queer self-love and wealth."

4. Take a sip from your goblet.

5. Now, with the music up, drink the rest of your holy wine while you use makeup, your mirror, and other glamour magick tools to look as extravagant as possible while expressing your unique gender identity.

6. Now, go to the club, orgy, or dance hall, and know that Dionysus is partying with and protecting you.

Resurrect Your Drag Persona

Drag doesn't change who you are, it actually reveals who you are.
—RuPaul[103]

You will need: Your epic playlist, a white candle, a lighter, a compass to find the directions (there's likely an app on your phone), your makeup, wigs, and favorite glamour supplies

The best time to cast the spell: Dark new moons, which represent new beginnings, are an excellent time to bring your drag persona to life.

Glamour witch says: Like any gender can be a witch, any gender can do drag. While traditionally when we think of drag, we think of gay men as drag queens, the scene is evolving. On *RuPaul's Drag Race*, Peppermint was the first transgender woman to compete in Season 9. Makeup artist Gottmik was the first transgender man to compete in Season 13. And the world is in desperate need of more drag kings, ladies.

Your drag persona already exists. We're going to resurrect them. Your drag persona is here to fuck with gender and bring to life the most authentic, high-octane version of yourself. Just like badass leather pairs perfectly with ballerina tulle, we're going to combine traditional elemental magick with makeup and mirrors to draw out your drag persona.

The Spell

1. Put on your loudest and proudest playlist with artists who embody your drag dreams. It's helpful to use a musician in your inspiration, as drag often includes lip-syncing, so you want to enjoy their music—even if you never plan to compete and are in this for fun.

2. Light a white candle to clear the energy while calling upon the elements.

3. With the candle in your hand, turn to the east. Say, "I call upon the drag royalty of the east, the element of air, or swift logic and intellect. Give me a sword to slay every last enemy."

4. Now turn to the south. Say, "I call upon the drag royalty of the south, the element of fire, of courage and passion. Give me a blazing wand, so I see myself on the stage in full glory."

5. Turn to the west. Say, "I call upon the drag royalty of the west, the element of water, of tears and psychic intuition. Give me a cup filled with creativity and empathy so I may find myself without drowning in fear."

6. Finally, turn to the north. Say, "I call upon the drag royalty of the north, the element of earth, of money and sensual comfort. Give me a solid foundation and chosen family to stand on so that I don't trip on the runway."

7. Now, bring your candle to your vanity, bathroom, or wherever you'll be going glam. Place it somewhere safe.

8. Now, go wild. This spell is a resurrection; it's OK to get messy. Crank up the music, play with makeup, try on wigs, even practice some poses. By the time your playlist is over, you'll already be reconnecting with your inner drag royalty.

7

GLAMOUR FOR PROTECTION
AND HEALING

The best revenge is massive success.

—Frank Sinatra[104]

Witches can be hurt unfortunately, and it's a mean, cruel world. As tarot teaches us, there is pain in life in addition to all of its wonders. Being a powerful glamour witch can incite jealousy. Sometimes even the most powerful of us get dick-matized and fall for someone who will only hurt us. That's why it's crucial to invest in your craft and, therefore, yourself.

This chapter helps you get your beauty sleep and reminds you that your bathtub is a cauldron waiting to brew up some self-care. But don't get it twisted; sometimes, you do need to show some teeth. So we'll also haunt enemies in their dreams, learn a mean poker face from tarot, and finally, utilize the moon to give mourning the respect it deserves while dressing to the nines.

Sleeping Beauty Ritual

You will need: Your preferred sleep attire, lavender essential oil

The best time to cast the spell: Right before bedtime

Glamour witch says: Sleep is crucial to your mental and physical well-being. So, after completing your nightly skin care ritual—and please, don't go to bed with your makeup on!—a glamour witch should approach the unconscious with the same attention that the waking hours get.

But we live in a stressful world, and ruminating thoughts can keep you up at night. Follow this beauty sleep ritual, which uses guided meditation, aromatherapy, and other sound sleep advice to slumber like Sleeping Beauty.

The Spell

1. First off, don't sleep on sleep glamour. Whether you prefer a beautiful silk nightgown, an oversize Nine Inch Nails T-shirt, or nothing at all, wear something comfortable to bed.

2. Screens are the nemesis of good sleep. Stay off your phone for at least the last hour before you go to bed.

3. Rub a small amount of lavender oil directly under your nose. The flower, which comes from the mint family, contains known calming properties, which can help you drift off to sleep.

4. Lying down in bed on your back in a room as dark as possible, begin a body scan. Start with your feet. Thank them for carrying you around all day. Imagine them growing heavy and sinking into the bed. Remind yourself that you are held and safe.

5. As you continue the body scan, breathe slowly and deeply, allowing the sedating lavender to fill your nostrils.

6. Move up to your legs. Thank them for everything they do for you, from dancing to looking fabulous in heels.

7. Continue up your body, curating your gratitude to your unique form until you reach your head. Tell yourself, "I am safe, I am loved, I am powerful." You can relax and let the tension leak out of your mind and into your nice, soft pillow.

8. Sweet dreams, beautiful.

Bath Magick for Self-Care

Whenever I'm sad I'm going to die, or so nervous I can't sleep, or in love with somebody I won't be seeing for a week, I slump down just so far and then I say: "I'll go take a hot bath."

—Sylvia Plath[105]

You will need: Candles, matches or a lighter, soothing playlist, ¾ cup Epsom salts with 3 ml or 120 drops of essential oils (or store-bought bath salts and bombs), a bathtub, a vibrator (optional)

The best time to cast the spell: Whenever you're feeling more stressed than blessed

Glamour witch says: Remember, glamour witches: your bathtub is a giant cauldron. Taking a bath is a recognized beauty ritual by people of all faiths. From Pagans to Christians, the act of baptism recognizes the renewing power of water. Sometimes, after a long day or when you're sick or in need of a mental health break, taking a bath can be the best thing for you. Epsom salts break down into magnesium and sulfate. When you soak in them, they can help relax muscles and stiff joints.

The Spell

1. Set an intention. It can simply be to relax, or it can be to wash off the day and prepare for a job interview in the morning.

2. Take your time to set up the proper atmosphere. Light candles and put on soothing music.

3. Get your bath glamour supplies ready. If you're making your own bath salts, mix ¾ cup Epsom salts with 3 ml or 120 drops of essential oils. Lavender is great for relaxation, and eucalyptus is an invigorating mood-booster.

4. Make sure your water is good and hot as you fill your bathtub. Hot water helps lower blood pressure, improve circulation, reduce stress, and allows you fall asleep easier.

5. If you're in the mood, grab a waterproof vibrator for orgasmic underwater fun. Or go old-fashioned and masturbate using the stream of bathwater. Orgasms are a natural mood-booster, as they release dopamine, serotonin, and oxytocin.

6. Add more magick to your bath with salts, bath bombs, and oils. Epsom salts alone relieve muscle tension and reduce swelling, whether it's from your home brew or store-bought for the busy witch. Companies such as Witch Baby even make bath bombs with crystals inside of them. So, if you want citrine in your bath to draw money, that can happen. If you're taking a bath for love—and feel free to invite your lover to join—opt for rose-scented beauty products, or go straight to the source and scatter your water with rose petals.

7. Soak until the water cools.

Sometimes using bath bombs and the like can make for extra cleanup, but trust me, it's worth it! Just imagine the cleanup if you choose to level up from water and bathe in champagne. Not only did Marilyn Monroe once bathe in hundreds of bottles of Piper-Heidsieck, but she'd also have a glass in the morning like one enjoys coffee.

Sparkling Social Media Shield

You will need: Yourself (put the phone away), a pillow or yoga mat, lepidolite

The best time to cast the spell: When the stress of social media is causing you anxiety or insecurities

Glamour witch says: Social media is like lip filler: a little bit can perform miracles, but too much is tragic. My friend the iconic publicist Melissa Vitale frequently warns her clients to "Stop listening to people who have more followers than money." (She's a Capricorn.) But honestly, it is a currency, and just like cash, you must learn how to wield it responsibly.

Social media helps you stay in touch with the world. During COVID-19, Instagram was basically how we showed everyone that we were alive and still capable—or not—of putting on makeup. And how else can we make fun of our high school friends' horrible husbands and gender reveal parties? It helps us show off our accomplishments, whether that's perfected eyeliner, a professional achievement, or the hot piece of ass that we're fucking. But speaking of professionals, some of us are required to use media for work and would commit professional suicide by deleting all of our accounts. But that doesn't mean that you can't implement social media breaks to stay sane. And, in addition to Muggle precautions, manifesting a protective shield for yourself can protect your mental health and sense of self from the fabrications of social media.

The Spell

1. Turn your cell phone off and put it in another room.

2. Sit somewhere comfortable, such as in front of your altar, on a pillow or yoga mat.

3. If you have lepidolite—a crystal that can be easily obtained online or at your local crystal shop—hold it in the palm of your hands. Lepidolite is a protective stone that eliminates electromagnetic pollution and other harmful technology vibes. Consider keeping one at your desk at all times.

4. Now imagine a diamond shield forming around your toes. It is sparkling, beautiful, and stunning.

5. Begin to chant the words: "Ancestors before me, and witches to come, keep me confident and protected from the negative effects of social media, so mote it be." As you chant these words, visualize your diamond shield moving up your legs, your torso, around your arms like armor, and above your head like a crown. You are now protected from online bullies and TikTok-induced insecurities from your toes to your tiara.

6. Keep your phone off for the rest of the night if you can. Whenever social media begins to stress you out, remind yourself of your diamond shield.

7. Repeat this ritual once a week or as needed.

P.S. Think of social media like your rising sign: it's the mask you present to the world. While it can be great fun to pretend that you don't have any zits, relationship problems, or financial woes, it also means that our enemies look fabulous, too. So, in addition to the spell above, please minimize stalking. It can warp your mind and spin you into a web of anxiety based on fake news. And unfollow or even block exes! While you're at it, unfollow their friends and family, too. You don't need that. Untag photos. Don't worry about what they will think; worry about what the next love of your life will think when they see that your Facebook is a museum dedicated to your ex. Always block and report bullies. They weren't cool on the playground, and they aren't cool now.

Haunt Their Dreams

You will need: Your glam arsenal (favorite outfits, hair, and makeup for the occasion), a pen and paper, and a mirror

The best time to cast the spell: At night when the object of your spell is asleep

Glamour witch says: They say that people are most vulnerable while they're sleeping. So, if you want to haunt a former lover or cruel boss, you can use mirror magick, glamour, and visualization to send them a message in their dreams.

The Spell

1. Get dressed to the nines. If there's something that connects to your spell target, such as a power suit or an outfit you wore on a big date, put that on. Do you want to enter their dreams smelling of roses in a pink tulle gown? Would you prefer to wear all black when you metaphorically stab them? The first step of this spell, honey, is to select your look!

2. Take a moment to reflect on the message that you wish to deliver. For example, maybe you want to tell your ex that you're hot and give them a wet dream about you. Or does your boss need to know that it's time for a raise? Write down your thoughts and condense them into one sentence.

3. Stand in front of your mirror. Visualize your target. What is their bedroom like? How are they sleeping? Get a visual that's so accurate it feels like you're there.

4. Stare at yourself right in the eye, like the bad bitch you are. Then, while maintaining your visualization, chant your message over and over until you feel like you've rid yourself of all the negative emotions attached.

5. Take off your makeup and go to bed, honey. Sleep in if you can. You deserve it!

The Emperor Poker Face

You will need: The Emperor card from a tarot deck

The best time to cast the spell: Tuesday, which is ruled by Mars, the god of war

Glamour witch says: There are times when it's helpful to conceal your emotions. For example, if you're terrified at a job interview, you don't necessarily want to show it. Additionally, while you should be honest about your feelings during important relationship talks, you want to keep cool. Witches tend to be overly empathetic and, as a result, can benefit from learning a poker face. Because a Lady Gaga reference is a must for this spell, yes, that includes fantasizing about a gender other than the person you're having sex with, as is the inspiration for the Aries's killer track.

Speaking of Aries, the tarot card that corresponds with the fire sign is the Emperor. Aries is the first sign of the zodiac and ruled by Mars, the god of war. The Emperor is a fatherlike authority figure that usually represents societal structure and rules. However, he's not some boring bureaucrat. Instead, the Emperor is a boss who knows how to command respect. If you can pull off a poker face with the Emperor, you can use it on anyone. After all, as Mars would agree, all is fair in love and war.

THE SPELL

1. Take out the Emperor from your favorite tarot deck. In the Rider-Waite-Smith deck, he's depicted as stern royalty, rocking a crown and a long white beard, and wearing red, the color of Aries and Mars.

2. Take a deep breath and clear your mind. Scrunch your face up to relieve tension in the muscles, and move into a calming state of mind.

3. Hold eye contact with the Emperor. Remember to blink, but not obsessively.

4. Stare straight ahead, even if he feels intimidating. Glancing all over the place can give away your nerves.

5. Practice asking a simple question that would arise during an intense conversation, using language which allows the other to speak. Choose your words carefully. Saying as little as possible and speaking in short, concise sentences can make keeping a power face easier. Ask the Emperor, "How are you feeling?"

6. While you look, keep your poker face, but listen. What is the Emperor trying to tell you? Often, this step can act as a mirror. You will likely find answers surrounding your insecurities while maintaining eye contact with the Emperor.

7. Put him back in the deck when it's time. Next up, kindly and compassionately practice your poker face in conversation.

Venus Immune Boost Tea

You will need: One slice of fresh ginger, one cup of water, a saucepan, one tablespoon of lemon juice, one teaspoon of apple cider vinegar, one tablespoon of raw honey, a mug

The best time to cast the spell: Anytime your immune system needs a loving boost

Glamour witch says: Whether you're healing from a new piercing or fending off a winter cold, every good witch should know how to whip up an immunity tea. This easy-to-make blend uses apple cider vinegar, lemon, ginger, and honey to give your immune system some love. And, remember, darlings, if you're sick, please rest. It's easy to feel pressure to work through illness these days, but you come first. Taking the time to heal is best for your body and helps you be more productive in the long run.

The Spell

1. Toss one slice of fresh ginger into one cup of water in a saucepan. Bring to a boil. Not only is ginger an anti-inflammatory, but it has antibacterial and antiviral properties. In spells, potent ginger is often used to boost personal power.

2. Add one tablespoon of lemon juice. Not only are lemons loaded with vitamin C, but they're associated with the prosperous sun, offering your body a dose of sunshine.

3. Add a teaspoon of apple cider vinegar. It contains acetic acid, which kills bacteria and helps your body fight off infections.

4. Finally, squeeze one heaping tablespoon of raw honey. Honey is often an offering to Venus, the goddess of love, abundance, and beauty. She wants you to feel better! Honey is also loaded with antioxidants and has both antifungal and antibacterial properties.

5. Pour the tea into a mug, let it cool, sip, and enjoy. And don't forget to rest!

Victorian Mourning Moon Ritual

You will need: Black, gray, and purple clothing

The best time to cast the spell: Over the course of one month, starting on the full moon

Glamour witch says: While the Victorians often frowned upon makeup, they knew what they were doing when it came to mourning practices. No one would dare tell a widow that she should stop wearing black already and move on in the Victorian era. While this mourning spell works after the death of a loved one, there does not need to be literal death to grieve. If you've recently gone through a breakup or had a falling out with a friend, allow yourself to experience the emotions

that change has caused you. Have you ever seen the Three of Swords?
Heartbreak hurts.

This spell is a modern take on Victorian fashion mourning rituals
following the moon's phases. While in the late 1800s in England, one
might wear hot layers of black for two years, this ritual uses an entire
moon cycle or a month to process. Of course, after that, it doesn't mean
that you are necessarily over your loss. But you have taken the time to
honor it.

The Spell

1. Full moons are primal and potent nights when the sky is alive with a cul-
mination. Right now, you may be feeling the searing pain or dull ache of
grief. That's OK. Put on some of your favorite black clothing. It can be nice
and comfy, or if you're mourning a breakup, as sexy as Princess Diana's
infamous "revenge dress."

2. Wear black for the next fourteen days during the entire waning phase of
the moon. When the moon is waning, it appears to become smaller in the
sky. This phase represents your grief gradually releasing you.

3. New moons are dark and intuitive times for fresh starts and new beginnings. This does not mean that you are done mourning, but you are starting to notice what's alive and worth celebrating. Remind yourself that just
because you lost something does not mean you lost the experience or yourself and how it helped you grow. And, if you are mourning a falling out with
a friend or family member, there is hope for eventual reconciliation. But
first, you must honor the hurt.

4. After the new moon, the waxing phase begins. The moon grows bigger and
brighter in the sky during this phase until it returns to a full moon. This
represents you reconnecting with yourself. Start to fade out black clothes
for poetic grays and purples, as the Victorians did. There is power in ritual
and color magick.

5. Once the next full moon arrives, feel free to return to your usual dress. Continue to take care of yourself and your mourning process with the support of friends, coven members, and a good therapist.

CONCLUSION

In 1938, a young Frank Sinatra was arrested for seduction. The charge meant that Ol' Blue Eyes had convinced a woman of good reputation to sleep with him. Perhaps, the authorities suspected, he hinted at marriage when that wasn't in the cards. However, it turned out that the woman was already married, and rather than drop the charges, they changed them to adultery.

This information was released to the public as part of a 1,300-page FBI file on Sinatra released in December 1998. The documents also contain information on his infamous mafia ties, friendship with John F. Kennedy, and the women, oh the women. He was married four times: to Nancy Barbato—the mother of his kids (although there are rumors that there are other love children)—Ava Gardner, Mia Farrow, and Barbara Marx. He also had relationships with Marilyn Monroe, Lana Turner, Judy Garland, and just about every other glamorous starlet of his era.

Yes, he was a playboy, but Sinatra felt life deeply. In 1953, when he was inconsolable due to his divorce from Gardner, he was found in the elevator of his Manhattan apartment with his wrists slashed. "I have an over-acute capacity for sadness as well as elation," Sinatra said in a 1950s interview. The detailed FBI file reveals that Sinatra got out of the draft because "[t]he examining psychiatrist concluded that this selectee suffered from psychoneurosis and was not acceptable material from the psychiatric viewpoint."

Sinatra was messy, problematic, and had a violent streak. However, he was also exceptionally talented, charismatic, and his artistic temperament and struggle with depression are relatable to anyone who's been called a witch. Singing about a temptress in the Grammy-winning 1957 tune "Witchcraft"—which Siouxsie Sioux would later perform in concert with her second band, The Creatures—Sinatra was undeniably a glamour witch himself. Perhaps, he got it from his mother.

Dolly Sinatra immigrated to New Jersey from Northern Italy when she was two years old. She worked with the local Democratic Party and is believed to have performed illegal abortions in addition to being a midwife. She gave birth to Frank on December 12, 1915—he's a Sagittarius—in a tenement in Hoboken. Frank was big from the beginning, literally. He weighed 13.5 pounds at birth and had to be delivered using forceps, causing severe scarring to his left cheek, neck, and ear and perforating his eardrum, which would be damaged for life and also helped him get out of the army. In addition, surgery on his mastoid bone left significant scarring on his neck, and during adolescence, he suffered from cystic acne that scarred his face and neck. "Don't hide your scars. They make you who you are," Frank once said.

Nevertheless, by all accounts, he was a devastatingly attractive man. "Frank attracted women. He couldn't help it. Just to look at him—the way he moved, and how he behaved—was to know that he was a great lover and true gentleman," said his fourth wife Barbara, whom he stayed with until his death. He also knew how to dress.

Frank looked the part from his teenage years singing with bands in New Jersey to the peak of his international fame. He performed only in impeccably tailored tuxedos and suits. "For me, a tuxedo is a way of life. When an invitation says black tie optional, it is always safer to wear black tie. My basic rules are to have shirt cuffs extended half an inch from the jacket sleeve. Trousers should break just above the shoe. Try not to sit down because it wrinkles the pants. If you have to sit, don't cross your legs. Pocket handkerchiefs are optional, but I always wear one, usually orange, since orange is my favorite color," Frank preached. If you recall, orange is the color associated with creativity, as notable in David Bowie's tangerine Ziggy Stardust days and the cover of Frank Ocean's epic album Channel Orange. Don't wear a brown suit at night; stick with black. Put on a fedora with two hands; Back brim curled up, front pulled down a couple of inches above the right brow. Be generous; tip well and discreetly. Such were just a few of Frank's glamour rules.

In 1995, Little Richard covered "That Old Black Magic" at Sinatra's eightieth birthday party. Sinatra loved it, and Little Richard had a chance to honor a man who greatly influenced his style. However, if Sinatra was glamour in black and white, Little Richard took that old black magic and turned on the color. He wore makeup, wigs, and shocked the system during the uptight era of the 1950s. After all, Little Richard wasn't just a man in flamboyant clothing, like Elvis. He was a queer Black man in capes and sequins. The original lyrics of his 1955 hit "Tutti Frutti" were: "Tutti Frutti, good booty / If it don't fit, don't force it / You can grease it, make it easy."

Little Richard struggled to reconcile his homosexuality with his Christian upbringing for most of his early life, although he found more peace with age. The same year he performed at Sinatra's birthday party, Little Richard told *Penthouse*, "I've been gay all my life and I know God is a God of love, not of hate." Later, he told GQ about going to orgies with all genders and described himself as "omnisexual," stating: "We are all both male and female. Sex to me is like a smörgåsbord. Whatever I feel like, I go for." Hex yeah.

However, Little Richard's wild onstage performances and dazzling outfits were more than self-expression or to put on a good show. They were a protection spell. "I wore makeup and wild outfits to keep white people from focusing on me as some kind of sexual threat," he told the *Wall Street Journal*. "I knew that if I looked crazy, not cool, I wouldn't be seen that way. And it worked. People focused on the music."

Throughout history, witches have always been the abortion doctors, the queer, the people of color, the different. As glamour witches, we can use the power costume, hair, and social media, not just graveyard dirt and bird skulls, as part of our craft. However, to be authentic glamour witches, we must understand that such persecution takes place within these mainstream tools. Sometimes a witch is an old hag in the woods, but others would use that word to describe the reproductive rights work of the woman who gave birth to Frank Sinatra. Yes, there are epic historical depictions of lesbians being accused of witchcraft for their secret dildos. Still, people like Little Richard managed to survive racist and homophobic attacks and become a legend. As you use your makeup brushes, tarot cards, and color schemes to level up your craft, keep your eyes open. Notice which designers made an effort to include diversity on the runway and who is stuck in the past. Pay attention to which hair salons offer services to all hair types and which ones don't even know what a Jheri curl is.

Your assignment is more than using glamour to feel beautiful. It's using these tools to become aware of your beauty. "I've been in this business for twenty years," Little Richard said on the *Dick Cavett Show* in 1970, "and I am the best-looking man in this business, without any doubt. I'm very, very beautiful. And I'm not conceited. I've never been conceited—I'm convinced . . . that I'm the best-looking thing." But more importantly, it's noticing the other glamour witches around you and promoting them, not persecuting them. Remember: As above, so below. Your glamour journey is most importantly about living in a manner that helps the world become a prettier place, too.

Notes

1. Colin Bertram, "David Bowie and Iman's Enduring Love Story," *Biography*, July 2, 2019, *biography.com*.

2. Guy Trebay, "Getting Personal with Iman," *New York Times*, November 18, 2021, *nytimes.com*.

3. "Glamour," Online Etymology Dictionary, accessed May 2022, *etymonline.com*.

4. Ray Rogers, "Beyonce Q&A: The Billboard Music Awards Millennium Artist Discusses Her Career And New Album," *Billboard*, March 11, 2022, *billboard.com*.

5. Tamar Gottesman, "Exclusive: Beyonce Wants to Change the Conversation," *Elle*, April 4, 2016, *elle.com*.

6. Dita Von Teese, *Your Beauty Mark: The Ultimate Guide to Eccentric Glamour* (New York: Dey Street Books, 2015).

7. "The History of 'Glamour,'" Word History on Merriam-Webster.com, accessed May 2022, *merriam-webster.com*.

8. Micaela Marini Higgs, "The Entirely False History of Women Tricking Men With Makeup," *Racked*, March 20, 2017, *racked.com*.

9. David Yi, *Pretty Boys: Legendary Icons Who Redefined Beauty and How to Glow Up, Too* (New York: Harper Design, 2021).

10. Tiffany M. Gill, *Beauty Shop Politics: African American Women's Activism in the Beauty Industry*, Women, Gender, and Sexuality in American History Series (Champaign: University of Illinois Press, 2010).

11. Matt Lavietes and Elliott Ramos, "Nearly 240 Anti-LGBTQ Bills Filed in 2022 So Far, Most of Them Targeting Trans People," NBC, March 20, 2022, *nbcnews.com*. Also visit Human Rights Campaign, *hrc.org*.

12. Jazz Jennings, *Being Jazz: My Life as a (Transgender) Teen* (South Bend, Ind.: Ember, 2017).

13. Thomas Laqueur, *Making Sex: Body and Gender from the Greeks to Freud* (Cambridge, Mass.: Harvard University Press, 1992).

14. Yi, *Pretty Boys*.

15. Laura Begley Bloom, "20 Most Dangerous Places For Gay Travelers (And The 5 Safest)," Forbes, November 25, 2019, *forbes.com*.

16. Human Rights Campaign, *hrc.org*.

17. Raisa Bruner, "Here's How Kristen Stewart Felt about Coming Out on SNL," *Time*, March 10, 2017, *time.com*.

18. "Social Order and Social Ordering in Stuart Ireland and Scotland," *Journal of Irish and Scottish Studies* 6(2) (spring 2013), *abdn.ac.uk*.

19. Eliza Thompson, "Here's Miley Cyrus Dressed as a Topless Rainbow Unicorn," *Cosmopolitan*, December 21, 2015, *cosmopolitan.com*.

20. ARN Radio, "Miley Cyrus Takes Shocking to Next Level with Strap-On Dildo," KIIS 1065, March 22, 2018, *kiis1065.com.au*.

21. Yi, *Pretty Boys*.

22. Human Rights Campaign, *hrc.org*.

23. Zachary Zane, "Everything to Know About the Bisexual Pride Flag," *Men's Health*, September 21, 2020, *menshealth.com*.

24. Jeanne Maglaty, "When Did Girls Start Wearing Pink?" *Smithsonian*, April 7, 2011, *smithsonianmag.com*.

25. Annabel Gat, *The Astrology of Love & Sex: A Modern Compatibility Guide* (New York: Chronicle, 2019).

26. Rachel Pollack, *Seventy-Eight Degrees of Wisdom: A Book of Tarot* (Newburyport, Mass.: Weiser Books, 2007).

27. Jillian Mapes, On Grimes, "We Appreciate Power," *Pitchfork*, November 29, 2018, *pitchfork.com*.

28. David Denicolo, "Alicia Keys on Makeup, Motherhood, and Her Musical Evolution," *Allure*, January 17, 2017, *allure.com*.

29. Elana Fishman, "Christian Louboutin and the Cardi B Effect," *Racked*, November 20. 2017, *racked.com*.

30. Alyssa Morin, "Everything You Need to Know about Florida Water, Solange's Witchy Met Gala Accessory," HelloGiggles, May 8, 2018, *hellogiggles.com*.

31. Aja Raden, *Stoned: Jewelry, Obsession, and How Desire Shapes the World* (New York: HarperCollins, 2015).

32. Harper's Bazaar Staff, "The 87 Greatest Fashion Quotes of All Time," *Harper's Bazaar*, February 3, 2022, *harpersbazaar.com*.

33. Doreen Valiente, *Witchcraft for Tomorrow* (London: Robert Hale Press, 1978).

34. Hollie McKay, "Gabourey Sidibe's Dress Mystery: When Plus Size Is Too Big for Hollywood," Fox News, April 11, 2016, *foxnews.com*.

35. Lauren Strapagiel, "Outing Is a Serious Threat to Trans People, and NikkieTutorials Isn't the First to Experience It," BuzzFeed.News, January 15, 2020, *buzzfeednews.com*.

36. Raden, *Stoned*.

37. Lance Hosey, "Why We Love Beautiful Things." *New York Times*, February 15, 2013, *nytimes.com*.

38. Forbes Quotes, "Thoughts on the Business of Life," *forbes.com*.

39. Meeta Jha, *The Global Beauty Industry: Colorism, Racism, and the National Body*, Framing 21st Century Social Issues (Milton Park, Oxfordshire, UK: Routledge, 2015).

40. Funmi Fetto, "How Fenty Beauty Changed the State of Play in the Industry," *Vogue*, April 6, 2020, *vogue.co.uk*.

41. Macaela Mackenzie, "Why Kylie Cosmetics' New Concealer Is Getting Criticized on Social Media Right Now," *Allure*, December 7, 2017, *allure.com*.

42. Gill, *Beauty Shop Politics*.

43. Tyffany Onyejiaka, "The Sunscreen Gap: Do Black People Need Sunscreen?" Healthline, September 27, 2019, *healthline.com*.

44. American Academy of Dermatology Association, "Sunscreen FAQs," AAD.org, accessed May 2022, *aad.org*; Roberta Schroeder, "This Is How Much Sunscreen You Should Be Applying to Your Face," *Harper's Bazaar*, March 21, 2021, *harpersbazaar.com*.

45. Andrew Jacono, *The Park Avenue Face: Secrets and Tips from a Top Facial Plastic Surgeon for Flawless, Undetectable Procedures and Treatments* (Dallas: BenBella Books, 2019).

46. Phoebe Robinson, *You Can't Touch My Hair: And Other Things I Still Have to Explain* (New York: Plume, 2016).

47. "'Break Their Lineage, Break Their Roots': China's Crimes against Humanity Targeting Uyghurs and Other Turkic Muslims," Human Rights Watch, April 19, 2021, *hrw.org*.

48. Chrissy Callahan, "Brittany Noble Jones Was Told Her Natural Hair Was 'Unprofessional' and Fired," *Today*, January 17, 2019, *today.com*.

49. Jessica Cruel, "The CROWN Act Makes Our Hair Just as Protected as Race, Sex, and Religious Beliefs," *Allure*, February 16, 2021, *allure.com*.

50. Yi, *Pretty Boys*.

51. Caitlin Maclead, "The Economics of the Human Hair Trade," *Hustle*, December 18, 2020, *thehustle.co*.

52. George Chauncey, *Gay New York: Gender, Urban Culture, and the Making of the Gay Male World, 1890–1940* (New York: Basic Books, 1994).

53. Erika Thomas, *Max Factor and Hollywood: A Glamorous History* (Charleston, S.C.: Arcadia Publishing, 2016).

54. Ruthie Fierberg, "How Long Does It Take to Turn Elphaba Green?" *Playbill*, July 12, 2017, *playbill.com*.

55. Brennan Kilbane, "The Business of Being Ariana Grande," *Allure*, October 2021, *allure.com*.

56. Yi, *Pretty Boys*.

57. ElectrikGlitter, *electrikglitter.com*.

58. Yi, *Pretty Boys*.

59. Matt Houlbrook, "'The Man with the Powder Puff' in Interwar London," *The Historical Journal* vol. 50, 1 (2007) *jstor.org*.

60. Jessica Pallingston, *Lipstick: A Celebration of the World's Favorite Cosmetic* (New York: Macmillan, 1999).

61. Von Teese, *Your Beauty Mark*.

62. Von Teese, *Your Beauty Mark*.

63. Hanna Flanagan, "Rihanna Celebrates Her Fenty Perfume Selling Out Hours After Launch with Caviar in Bed, *People*, August 10, 2021, *people.com*.

64. Yi, Pretty Boys.

65. *Les Secrets de Maistre Alexys* (Venice 1555).

66. Thatiana Diaz, "Super Bowl Star Bad Bunny on Fighting Gender Norms with Nail Art," *Refinery29*, February 3, 2020, *refinery29.com*.

67. Patricia Tortolani, "Bad Bunny Is Here at the Right Time," *Allure*, November 2021, *allure.com*.

68. Olivia Jakiel, "Gwen Stefani's New Music Video Is Raising Eyebrows. Here's Why," *The List*, April 9, 2021, *thelist.com*.

69. UN/DN Laqr, *undnlaqr.com*.

70. Lauren Valenti, "From David Bowie to Bad Bunny, the Famous Men Who Have Made Nail Art Their Beauty Signature," *Vogue*, May 9, 2022, *vogue.com*.

71. Rachel Krause, "You Won't Believe Where the French Manicure Is Actually From," *Refinery29*, April 26, 2018, *refinery29.com*.

72. Hannah Yasharoff, "Dolly Parton Isn't Afraid to Talk Plastic Surgery: 'I Look Artificial' But I'm Still Real," *USA Today*, September 3, 2019, *usatoday.com*.

73. Emily Jane Fox, "Melania Trump Opens Up About Botox and Getting Donald's Number," *Vanity Fair*, April 27, 2016, *vanityfair.com*.

74. Coby Michael, *The Poison Path Herbal: Baneful Herbs, Medicinal Nightshades, and Ritual Entheogens* (Rochester, Vt.: Park Street Press, 2021).

75. Nikkie de Jager, Twitter post, July 1, 2018, 6:10PM, *twitter.com*.

76. Joan Rivers Quotes, BrainyQuote.com, BrainyMedia Inc, 2022, accessed June 17, 2022, *brainyquote.com*.

77. Yi, *Pretty Boys*.

78. Janet Mock, *Redefining Realness: My Path to Womanhood, Identity, Love & So Much More* (New York: Atria Books, 2014).

79. Tony Enos, "8 Things You Should Know about Two Spirit People," *Indian Country Today*, September 13, 2018, indiancountrytoday.com.

80. Trudy Ring, "Here Are the 57 Trans Americans Killed in 2021," *The Advocate*, October 20, 2021, advocate.com.

81. "Gender Affirmation (Confirmation) or Sex Reassignment Surgery," Cleveland Clinic, accessed June 20, 2022, my.clevelandclinic.org.

82. Jake Hall, "The Real Deal: An Honest Interview with Brooke Candy," *The Face*, June 20, 2019, theface.com.

83. Tyler M. Schwaller, "The Use of Slaves in Early Christianity: Slaves as Subjects of Life and Thought" (dissertation, Harvard, 2017), dash.harvard.edu.

84. Albert Parry, *Tattoo: Secrets of a Strange Art* (Mineola, N.Y.: Dover Publications, 2006).

85. American Society for Aesthetic Plastic Surgery, physiciansaestheticcoalition.org.

86. Elayne Angel, *The Piercing Bible: The Definitive Guide to Safe Piercing* (Emeryville, Calif.: Ten Speed Press, 2021).

87. Kate Freuler, "Working with Bones and Skulls in Witchcraft," *Llewellyn*, July 6, 2020, llewellyn.com.

88. Georgy Manaev, "The mystery of the Siberian Ice Maiden," *Russia Beyond*, May 31, 2021, rbth.com.

89. Grant Stoddard, "People Are Shoving Beads into Their Penis Skin for Better Sex," *Vice*, July 30, 2018, vice.com.

90. Stephen Kern, *Anatomy and Destiny: A Cultural History of the Human Body* (Indianapolis: Bobbs-Merrill Company, 1st edition, 1975).

91. Fakir Musafar Foundation, "May 2018: A Farewell Message from Fakir," fakir.org.

92. Daniel E. Slotnik, "Fakir Musafar, Whose 'Body Play' Went to Extremes, Dies at 87," *New York Times*, August 13, 2018, nytimes.com.

93. "Self-Harm," NAMI, accessed May 2022, nami.org.

94. Meagan Angus, "The History and Possibilities of Putting Weed in Your Witchcraft," *Seattle Weekly*, June 28, 2017, seattleweekly.com.

95. "Recipe: How to make basic cannabis-infused butter," Leafly, March 25, 2020, leafly.com.

96. Jacono, *The Park Avenue Face*.

97. Suzy Nightingale, "These 5 Tricks Help Your Fragrance Last Longer . . . ," The Perfume Society, accessed May 2022, perfumesociety.org.

98. Natalie Keegan, "Eye've Always Wondered: This Is the Reason Why We Wish on Eyelashes . . . It's Actually Pretty Sinister," *The Sun*, April 2, 2017, thesun.co.uk.

99. Tiffany Aliche, *Get Good with Money: Ten Simple Steps to Becoming Financially Whole* (Emmaus, Penn.: Rodale Books, 2021).

100. Erica Euse, "There's a Reason You Cut Your Hair After a Breakup," *i-D Magazine*, June 12, 2018, vice.com.

101. Cassandra Snow, *Queering the Tarot* (Newburyport, Mass.: Weiser Books, 2019).

102. Siobhan, "Let's Talk About Dionysys: Genderqueer God of Partying and Pride," Autostraddle, May 16, 2017, autostraddle.com.

103. Yi, *Pretty Boys*.

104. Frank Sinatra Quotes, BrainyQuote.com, BrainyMedia Inc, 2022, accessed June 17, 2022, brainyquote.com.

105. Sylvia Plath, *The Bell Jar* (New York: Harper Perennial Modern Classics, 2005).

References

Aftel, Mandy. *Essence and Alchemy: A Natural History of Perfume.* Berkeley, Calif.: Aftel Perfumes, 2004.

Angel, Elayne. *The Piercing Bible: The Definitive Guide to Safe Piercing.* Trumansburg, N.Y.: Crossing Press, 2009.

Fearon, Faye. "Eight Times Frank Sinatra Mastered Proper Masculine Elegance." *GQ,* December 12, 2019, *gq-magazine.co.uk.*

Gat, Annabel. *The Astrology of Love & Sex: A Modern Compatibility Guide.* New York: Chronicle, 2019.

Gilbert, Steve. *Tattoo History: A Source Book.* New York: Juno Books, 2000.

Gill, Tiffany M. *Beauty Shop Politics: African American Women's Activism in the Beauty Industry Space.* Champaign: University of Illinois Press, 2010.

Gladstone, India. "Frank Sinatra's defining style moments." *Gentleman's Journal,* accessed May 2022, *thegentlemansjournal.com.*

Glucklich, Ariel. *Sacred Pain: Hurting the Body for the Sake of the Soul.* Oxford, UK: Oxford University Press, 2003.

Hall, Judy. *The Crystal Bible: A Definitive Guide to Crystals.* Iola, Wisc.: Krause Publications, 2003.

Hernandez, Gabriela. *Classic Beauty: The History of Makeup.* Atglen, Penn.: Schiffer, 2017.

Jacono, Andrew. *The Park Avenue Face: Secrets and Tips from a Top Facial Plastic Surgeon for Flawless, Undetectable Procedures and Treatments.* Dallas: BenBella Books, 2019.

Malone, Chris. "A Brief History of Little Richard Grappling with His Sexuality & Religion." *Billboard,* October 9, 2017, *billboard.com.*

Meeta Rani Jha. *The Global Beauty Industry: Colorism, Racism, and the National Body.* Abington, Oxfordshire, UK: Routledge, 2016.

Myers, Marc. "Richard, the First." *Wall Street Journal,* August 10, 2010, *wsj.com.*

Okwodu, Janelle. "Little Richard Changed the Course of Fashion History Too." *Vogue*, May 11, 2020, *vogue.com*.

Philippon, Laurent. *Hair: Fashion and Fantasy*. London: Thames & Hudson, 2013.

Pollack, Rachel. *Seventy-Eight Degrees of Wisdom: A Book of Tarot*. Newburyport, MA: Weiser Books, 2007.

Raden, Aja. *Stoned: Jewelry, Obsession, and How Desire Shapes the World*. New York: HarperCollins, 2015.

Rhea, Lady. *The Enchanted Candle: Crafting and Casting Magickal Light*. New York: Citadel, 2004.

Saint Thomas, Sophie. "A Witch's Guide to Cord Cutting, the Simple Ritual to Get Over Your Ex." *Vice*, February 15, 2019, *vice.com*.

Saint Thomas, Sophie. *Finding Your Higher Self: Your Guide to Cannabis for Self-Care*. Avon, MA.: Adams Media, 2019.

Watson, Linda. *Vogue Fashion: Over 100 Years of Style by Decade and Designer*. Richmond Hill, ON: Firefly Books, 2008.

Yi, David. *Pretty Boys: Legendary Icons Who Redefined Beauty and How to Glow Up, Too*. New York: Harper Design, 2021.

About the Author

Sophie Saint Thomas, originally from the Virgin Islands, is an acclaimed queer sex writer and witch living in New York City. She has been a columnist for *VICE*, a producer at MTV Networks, and is currently a full-time freelance writer. She has contributed to *GQ, Allure, Glamour, Marie Claire, PRIDE, Cosmopolitan, Harper's Bazaar, Playboy, Noisey, High Times, Refinery29, Mic,* and *Nylon,* among others. She is the resident astrologer at *Allure* and writes the sex column "Never Have I Ever" for *AskMen*. This is her fourth book. Follow Sophie @thebowiecat.

To Our Readers

Weiser Books, an imprint of Red Wheel/Weiser, publishes books across the entire spectrum of occult, esoteric, speculative, and New Age subjects. Our mission is to publish quality books that will make a difference in people's lives without advocating any one particular path or field of study. We value the integrity, originality, and depth of knowledge of our authors.

Our readers are our most important resource, and we appreciate your input, suggestions, and ideas about what you would like to see published.

Visit our website at *www.redwheelweiser.com*, where you can learn about our upcoming books and free downloads, and also find links to sign up for our newsletter and exclusive offers.

You can also contact us at *info@rwwbooks.com* or at

Red Wheel/Weiser, LLC
65 Parker Street, Suite 7
Newburyport, MA 01950